Empowered to Serve

by
John MacArthur, Jr.

MOODY PRESS
CHICAGO

All Scripture quotations, unless noted otherwise, are from the *New Scofield Reference Bible*, King James Version. Copyright © 1967 by Oxford University Press, Inc. Reprinted by permission.

Library of Congress Cataloging in Publication Data

MacArthur, John F.
  Empowered to serve.

  (John MacArthur's Bible studies)
  Includes indexes.
  1. Bible.   N.T.   Acts I, 1-II, 13—Criticism, inter-
pretation, etc.   I. Title.   II. Series: MacArthur,
John F.   Bible studies.
BS2625.2.M26   1987   226'.607   87-11066
ISBN 0-8024-5314-7

1 2 3 4 5 6 7 Printing/LC/Year 91 90 89 88 87

Printed in the United States of America

Contents

These Bible studies are taken from messages delivered by Pastor-Teacher John MacArthur, Jr., at Grace Community Church in Panorama City, California. The recorded messages themselves may be purchased as a series or individually. Please request the current price list by writing to:

WORD OF GRACE COMMUNICATIONS
P.O. Box 4000
Panorama City, CA 91412

Or call the following number:
818-982-7000

1
Resources for Finishing
Our Lord's Unfinished Work—Part 1

Outline

Introduction
A. The Writer
B. The Recipient
   1. The purpose
   2. The person

Lesson
 I. The Proper Message (vv. 1-2)
    A. Taught by the Example of Christ
       1. Learning from Christ's teaching
       2. Learning from Christ's actions
    B. Taught by the Empowerment of the Spirit
    C. Taught to the Elect of God
 II. The Proper Manifestation (v. 3)
    A. Christ Increased the Apostles' Faith (v. 3a)
    B. Christ Increased the Apostles' Knowledge (v. 3b)
III. The Proper Might (vv. 4-5, 8a)
    A. The Petition (v. 4)
       1. The necessity of Jesus' departure
       2. The necessity of the Spirit's arrival
    B. The Prediction (v. 5)
    C. The Promise (v. 8a)

Introduction

These lessons are a study of Acts 1:1–2:13. Before we get into our study, however, I want to give some background information about the book of Acts.

A. The Writer

Acts 1:1 says, "The former treatise have I made, O Theophilus, of all that Jesus began both to do and teach." In an indirect way, that verse tells us who wrote the book of Acts. Luke 1:3-4 says, "It seemed good to me also, having had perfect understanding of all things from the very first, to write unto thee in order, most excellent Theophilus, that thou mightest know the certainty of those things, wherein thou hast been instructed." Luke wrote his gospel for Theophilus. Then when he wrote a sequel—the book of Acts—for Theophilus, he referred to his gospel as "the former treatise" (Acts 1:1).

Luke is not mentioned often in the New Testament. He appears in three verses: Colossians 4:14, 2 Timothy 4:11, and Philemon 24. Consequently, little is known about him. Colossians tells us he was a medical doctor. That is corroborated by the medical terminology he used in his gospel as well as by some of the situations he wrote about. Second Timothy says he was a companion to the imprisoned apostle Paul. The context of the Colossians reference suggests Luke was a Gentile—making him perhaps the only Gentile writer of the New Testament.

B. The Recipient

1. The purpose

The book of Acts was addressed to Theophilus. Because Luke referred to his gospel as "the former treatise," we can consider Acts to be the second volume of Luke's writings. In the gospel of Luke he told us about the works and teachings of Jesus Christ (Acts 1:1). Then in Acts he picked up where the gospel of Luke left off by speaking of Christ's ascension and the coming of the Holy Spirit.

2. The person

The name *Theophilus* is a combination of two Greek words. It means "beloved of God" or "friend of God." Little is known about him. Second-century sources indicate he was a wealthy, influential official in Antioch. Luke may have also been from Antioch, which would explain how the two men got to know each other.

Theophilus was a Roman citizen who was a believer. He may have been a high-ranking Roman official because Luke referred to him as "most excellent Theophilus" (Luke 1:3). The term *excellent* is also used in the Bible in reference to Felix and Festus, who were Roman governors (Acts 23:26; 26:25).

Is Christ's Work Finished or Not?

Luke says in Acts 1:1, "The former treatise have I made, O Theophilus, of all that Jesus *began* to do and teach" (emphasis added). The word *began* implies that Christ's work on earth was not finished, yet in His high priestly prayer to His Father, Jesus said, "I have finished the work which thou gavest me to do" (John 17:4). When He died on the cross He said, "It is finished" (John 19:30). The reason Luke said Christ's work had begun is because he was referring to the work of evangelism and teaching. Christ's redemptive work on the cross *is* done, but the work of teaching God's Word is not. We are to continue teaching the gospel message of Christ. That's why I titled this lesson "Resources for Finishing Our Lord's Unfinished Work."

As we study Acts 1:1–2:13, keep in mind that Luke is writing about a great transition. Jesus did almost all the gospel teaching up to the time of His death and resurrection. The disciples hadn't done much teaching; their experience was probably limited to the time Jesus sent them out in Matthew 10. But before Christ ascended, He gave to the disciples the responsibility of evangelizing the world. From a human standpoint, they weren't highly qualified individuals. But Christ was about to equip them so that they would be able to carry out His work.

In Acts 1 we see seven things that the Lord did to prepare His disciples for their work: He taught them (the proper message), appeared to them (the proper manifestation), empowered them (the proper might), hid a mystery from them (the proper mystery), commissioned them (the proper mission), gave a promise to them (the proper motive), and replaced a traitor (the proper men).

Lesson

I. THE PROPER MESSAGE (vv. 1-2)

"The former treatise have I made, O Theophilus, of all that Jesus began both to do and teach, until the day in which he was taken up, after he, through the Holy Spirit, had given commandments unto the apostles whom he had chosen."

A. Taught by the Example of Christ

   1. Learning from Christ's teaching

      To effectively carry on the Lord's work, you need to know the proper message. There's no sense in trying to preach the gospel if you don't have the right information. Acts 1:1-2 says that Christ taught the apostles right up until the time He ascended into heaven.

Preparing for Ministry

If you are thinking about going into some type of Christian ministry that requires teaching or evangelizing, you need to be trained. You can't just say, "I'm ready; I'm going to go out into the world and tell everyone what I know about Christ." You will run out of things to say if you're not adequately prepared. I've known people who have rushed into some type of ministry and run out of things to do after a while. It's necessary to fill your mind with the facts before any kind of ministry can be effective.

People ask me why I spent so much time in school before I became a pastor. Without that schooling I would not have been equipped to teach God's Word. Every year I spent in school and every paper I wrote contributed to my preparation for ministry. We need to know God's Word before we can share it with others; there's no substitute for that. Hosea said, "My people are destroyed for lack of knowledge" (4:6). One of the greatest problems in the church today is ignorance. Some people who have gone to church for ten or twenty years know next to nothing about the Bible. God doesn't tolerate ignorance; 2 Timothy 2:15 says, "Study to show thyself approved unto God." Take the time to get the facts straight—it's worth it.

2. Learning from Christ's actions

Having the proper knowledge isn't all that's necessary; you need to apply what you learn every day. Luke wrote his gospel to tell of "all that Jesus began both to *do* and teach" (emphasis added). The word *do* appears before the word *teach*. That's because you can teach biblical principles only when you are living them. You can't teach on a matter or subject that you have no experience with. If you want to carry on Jesus' work, you need more than an intellectual awareness of the facts; you need to be living out what you teach.

The religious leaders of Israel appeared to be the most righteous people of all, yet Jesus said, "The scribes and the Pharisees sit in Moses' seat. All, therefore, whatever they bid you observe, that observe and do; but do not after their works; for they say, and do not" (Matt. 23:2-3). The Pharisees didn't live by what they taught. The same goes for today; there's a lack of powerful preaching today because some teachers are ignorant about what the Bible teaches or because they don't apply what they know.

If your knowledge of God's Word isn't transforming your own life, don't expect it to transform the lives of others. There are ministers who preach the Word yet live in sin. When their sin is exposed, the congregation is in turmoil because they see the contradiction between the minister's words and his actions. Nineteenth-century Scottish preacher Robert Murray McCheyne wrote this to a fellow minister: "Remember you are God's sword, His instrument. . . . In great measure according to the purity and perfections of the instrument, will be the success. It is not great talents God blesses so much as great likeness to Jesus. A holy minister is an awful weapon in the hand of God" (*Memoirs of McCheyne*, Andrew A. Bonar, ed. [Chicago: Moody, 1947], p. 95).

You must be living God's Word before you can teach it. Jesus did that up to the time He was taken to heaven. Several times He said He would return to heaven (John 6:62; 16:28; 20:17), but before He did that He carefully taught the disciples and showed them the divine pattern for living.

B. Taught by the Empowerment of the Spirit

Acts 1:2 says that Christ gave His commandments to the apostles "through the Holy Spirit." Although it was Christ—the second Person of the Trinity—who came to earth to minister to mankind, His ministry was accomplished through the power of the Holy Spirit. Christ also said He came to do the will of the Father (John 4:34). So all three Persons of the Trinity were involved in Christ's work on earth. Yet the religious leaders of Israel didn't recognize that. After seeing Christ do the miraculous, they concluded that He was empowered by the devil (Matt. 12:24). They were blinded by their sin. Jesus told them that if they spoke against Him they could be forgiven, but because they were denying what the Spirit was doing through Him, they had blasphemed the Holy Spirit and committed an unpardonable sin (Matt. 12:31-32).

Why did the Trinity choose for Jesus to be empowered through the Holy Spirit? I think because Jesus was setting a pattern for us to follow. All that we do for God, including teaching the gospel message, is to be done in the power of the Spirit.

C. Taught to the Elect of God

Acts 1:2 says Christ "had given commandments unto the apostles whom *he had chosen*" (emphasis added). Jesus chose His own missionaries, taught them, and commissioned them with certain responsibilities. The same is true of all Christians: we are chosen by Christ. John 15:16 says,

"Ye have not chosen me, but I have chosen you, and ordained you, that ye should go and bring forth fruit."

To be an effective teacher or evangelist for Christ, you have to be saturated with God's Word. Nineteenth-century English preacher Charles H. Spurgeon said that we might preach until our tongues rotted, until we exhaust our lungs and die—but never a soul would be converted unless the Holy Spirit uses the Word to convert it. He said we're to delve into the very heart of the Bible until at last we come to talk in scriptural language and our spirits are flavored with the words of the Lord, so that the very essence of the Bible flows from us. I hope you are actively taking in God's Word and pouring it out to others.

II. THE PROPER MANIFESTATION (v. 3)

"To whom also he showed himself alive after his passion by many infallible proofs, being seen by them forty days, and speaking of the things pertaining to the kingdom of God."

A. Christ Increased the Apostles' Faith (v. 3a)

Christ appeared only to His chosen ones, not to unbelievers. The purpose of that was to prepare the apostles for their ministry to unbelievers. Rather than try to work with unbelievers Himself, Christ empowered others to do the job, and that's what He does with us now.

It was important for the apostles to know that Jesus is a risen Lord. Who wants to go around propagating the gospel of a dead leader? Christ showed Himself to the apostles so they would know He had conquered death. One of the greatest proofs of the resurrection is the early church's boldness and commitment in preaching about Christ. The apostles were confident because they had seen Christ in His resurrection glory. Had that not happened, they would have gone back to the routine of life and quit advocating Christianity. But Christ appeared to the apostles repeatedly over a period of forty days to confirm that He was a risen, glorified Messiah.

There is a list of all the people Christ appeared to in 1 Corinthians 15:5-8. Those appearances convinced Christ's followers that the Lord had indeed risen. When the resurrected Christ asked His disciples to dine with Him at the Sea of Galilee, "none of the disciples dared ask him, Who art thou? knowing that it was the Lord" (John 21:12).

B. Christ Increased the Apostles' Knowledge (v. 3b)

What did Christ do when He appeared to the apostles? He spoke to them "of the things pertaining to the kingdom of God" (Acts 1:3). Before Christ died, He taught frequently about God's future kingdom, and did the same after His resurrection. That must have encouraged the apostles because now they knew for certain that the promises regarding God's future kingdom would come true. If Christ had never risen, they would have thought there was no hope for a future kingdom. They would have wondered, *How can there be a kingdom someday when the leader of that kingdom is dead?* But Christ arose, and that restored the apostles' confidence in preaching about the coming kingdom.

How does Acts 1:3 apply to us? We have not seen Jesus with our eyes, but He has manifested Himself to us. The apostle Paul didn't see Christ physically, but in 1 Corinthians 9:1 he says that he saw Him. How? With his spiritual eye. Jesus says in John 20:29, "Blessed are they that have not seen, and yet have believed." We don't need to see Jesus with our physical eyes; we can see Him with the eyes of faith. I'd rather have Christ present with us spiritually than physically. In a physical body, Christ was limited to doing His work in the locations He traveled to. But with His Spirit inside us, He can work through all Christians everywhere. First Corinthians 12:3 says, "No man can say that Jesus is the Lord, but by the Holy Spirit." It's the Spirit who reveals Christ to us. Jesus told the disciples, "When the Comforter [the Holy Spirit] is come, whom I will send unto you from the Father, even the Spirit of truth, who proceedeth from the Father, he shall testify of me" (John 15:26). Christ is present in your life, and He manifests Himself through you so that you might know He's alive. His presence gives us confidence when we preach about Him. First Peter 1:8 says we love Him even though we can't see Him. Christ is real to us.

III. THE PROPER MIGHT (vv. 4-5, 8a)

A. The Petition (v. 4)

"[Christ] being assembled together with them [the apostles], commanded them that they should not depart from Jerusalem, but wait for the promise of the Father, which, saith he, ye have heard from me."

Even though the disciples had been taught by Christ and knew He had risen from the dead, they still weren't ready to go out and win people. Christ had told them to go out and teach all nations (Matt. 28:20), but in Acts 1:4 He adds that they shouldn't yet depart from Jerusalem. He said, "Wait for the promise of the Father, which . . . ye have heard from me." Jesus says the same thing in Luke 24:49: "Behold, I send the promise of my Father upon you; but tarry ye in the city of Jerusalem, until ye be endued with power from on high."

What was the "promise of the Father" that He had told them about? The gift of the Holy Spirit. Jesus told the apostles they would receive the Holy Spirit after He left them (John 14:16, 26; 15:26; 16:7; 20:22). Acts 2:33 confirms that the Father sent the Holy Spirit once Christ was at His right hand in heaven.

1. The necessity of Jesus' departure

Jesus tells the apostles in John 16:7, "It is expedient for you that I go away; for if I go not away, the Comforter will not come unto you; but if I depart, I will send him unto you." The Spirit couldn't be sent until Christ returned to heaven. The disciples had to wait ten days between the ascension and the day they received the Spirit, the Day of Pentecost (Acts 2:1). *Pentecost* is Greek for "the fiftieth day." It was the day the Jewish people celebrated the feast of harvest and fell on the fiftieth day after the feast of Passover. It also refers to the fifty-day period between Christ's resurrection and the sending of the Spirit.

2. The necessity of the Spirit's arrival

The apostles had to receive the Holy Spirit before they could do the Lord's work. That shows us that it's impossible to carry on His work in our own power. You can make elaborate plans for ministry and give eloquent sermons, but without the Spirit's power your work will be fruitless. The apostles themselves knew they needed the Spirit's power. When Christ first commissioned them to spread the gospel, He said, "It is not ye that speak, but the Spirit of your Father who speaketh in you" (Matt. 10:20). In Luke 12:12 the apostles were told there would come a day when the Spirit would speak through them. John 14:17 says that the Holy Spirit was already with the disciples, but that later on He would be in them. (Prior to the sending of the Spirit in Acts 2, people weren't indwelt by the Holy Spirit. Instead, God sent the Spirit on specific occasions to do a special work through someone. For example, the Holy Spirit descended on King Saul [1 Sam. 11:6] and departed from him [1 Sam. 16:14]).

B. The Prediction (v. 5)

"For John truly baptized with water; but ye shall be baptized with the Holy Spirit not many days from now."

Before Jesus began His public ministry, John the Baptist said of Him, "I baptize with water; but there standeth one among you, whom ye know not. . . . He that sent me to baptize with water, the same said unto me, Upon whom thou shalt see the Spirit descending and remaining on him, the same is he who baptizeth with the Holy Spirit. And I saw, and bore witness that this is the Son of God" (John 1:26, 33-34). Jesus is the One who baptizes with the Holy Spirit, and the disciples had to wait in Jerusalem until He sent the Spirit from heaven.

The disciples were going to receive their baptism in ten days (Christ's command for the disciples to wait for the Spirit was given on the day of His ascension, which was forty days after the resurrection. The Spirit came on the

Day of Pentecost, which was fifty days after the resurrection, thus making the wait ten days.) Now that doesn't mean a person receives the Spirit ten days after he becomes saved. The situation in Acts was unique; Jesus hadn't ascended to heaven yet to send the Holy Spirit. Now every believer receives the Spirit the moment He receives Christ as Savior. Romans 8:9 says, "If any man have not the Spirit of Christ, he is none of his." A person without the Holy Spirit isn't a Christian.

C. The Promise (v. 8a)

"Ye shall receive power, after the Holy Spirit is come upon you."

Prior to receiving the Holy Spirit, the apostles were powerless to carry out Christ's unfinished work. The Greek word translated "power" (*dunamis*) is the source of our English word *dynamite*. Every Christian is packed with power—the Holy Spirit.

Some Christians feel they are lacking in power. If you feel like that, it's not God's fault. The power is within you. All you need to do is turn on the ignition switch. How is that done? Ephesians 5:18 says, "Be not drunk with wine, in which is excess, but be filled with the Spirit." A simple way to illustrate the filling of the Spirit is with Alka-Seltzer tablets. Within each tablet is a concentrated form of medication that is released when put into a glass of water. Likewise, the Person of the Holy Spirit is like a concentrated form of energy within you. The power is in you, but you need to release it and allow it to permeate your life.

To live a Spirit-filled life means to yield yourself to the control of the Spirit. In the Bible, the word *filled* is primarily used in connection with a particular attitude. It is used to speak of being filled with rage, anger, sorrow, or faith. Whatever the person is filled with overrides other emotions or attitudes. Someone filled with sorrow is overwhelmed with sorrow. Someone filled with the Spirit is allowing the Spirit to control his life. It's one thing to possess the Spirit, yet another to be filled by Him.

How Can I Let the Holy Spirit Fill My Life?

The answer is in Colossians 3:16: "Let the word of Christ dwell in you richly." Being filled with the Holy Spirit and letting the Word of Christ dwell in you richly are synonymous because they produce the same results. When you are filled with the Spirit, you will have a song in your heart, be thankful, love your spouse and children, and serve your employer well (Eph. 5:19–6:9). The same is true for letting the Word of Christ dwell in you richly (Col. 3:16–4:1).

To let the Word of Christ dwell in you richly is to be preoccupied with the presence of Christ. The more you saturate your mind with what you learn about Him from the Bible, the more He controls your thoughts. By yielding yourself totally to the Word of God and letting it permeate your life, you'll be controlled by the Spirit's desires and not your own.

God can do great things through you. Ephesians 3:20 says the Lord is able to do "exceedingly abundantly above all that we ask or think, according to the power that worketh in us." The power is in you; it just needs to be released. That happens when you yield every aspect of your life to the Spirit's control.

Focusing on the Facts

1. What was Luke's purpose in writing the book of Acts (Acts 1:1; see p. 8)?
2. What work has Christ already finished? What work must we continue to carry on (see p. 9)?
3. Why is knowledge of Scripture so important for ministry (see pp. 10-11)?
4. With what does knowledge need to be supplemented (see p. 11)?
5. Why is there a lack of powerful preaching today (see p. 11)?
6. To be an _____ teacher or evangelist for Christ, you have to be _____ with God's Word (see p. 13).
7. To whom did Christ appear after His resurrection? Why (see p. 13)?
8. What did Christ do when He appeared to the apostles after His resurrection? What effect did that have on the apostles (see p. 14)?

9. What command did Christ give the apostles in Acts 1:4? Why (see p. 15)?
10. What does Romans 8:9 say about a person in relation to the Holy Spirit (see p. 17)?
11. What does every Christian possess (see p. 17)?
12. What does it mean to live a Spirit-filled life (see p. 17)?
13. How can you let the Holy Spirit fill your life (see p. 18)?

Pondering the Principles

1. What are you doing right now to assure that you develop a thorough knowledge of God's Word? The range of possibilities is wide: you can commit yourself to a daily Bible-reading schedule, take notes during Sunday services or Bible study meetings, read good Christian books, be discipled by a mature Christian, take classes or a correspondence course with a Christian college, subscribe to a Christian magazine, or listen to good Christian teachers on television or radio. Make sure you are receiving nourishment daily from God's Word using one or more of those avenues for learning. The best way to do that is to meet regularly with a good Christian friend to share with each other what you're learning so that you may "grow in grace, and in the knowledge of our Lord and Savior, Jesus Christ" (2 Pet. 3:18).

2. Christ came to earth to reveal God to mankind. He did that not only through His words but His actions as well. Get together with a Christian friend and discuss what practical applications you can make for your own attitudes and actions based on Christ's example: Mark 6:34, John 17:20-23, Philippians 2:5-8, and 1 Peter 2:21-23. When you follow Christ's pattern in your life, you will be rewarded with the blessings that come from living in accord with God's will.

2
Resources for Finishing Our Lord's Unfinished Work—Part 2

Outline

Introduction

Review
 I. The Proper Message (vv. 1-2)
 II. The Proper Manifestation (v. 3)
   A. Christ Increased the Apostles' Faith (v. 3*a*)
   B. Christ Increased the Apostles' Knowledge (v. 3*b*)
     1. The universal kingdom of God
     2. The mediatorial kingdom of God
       a) Ruling through man's conscience
       b) Ruling through human government
       c) Ruling through the patriarchs
       d) Ruling through the judges, prophets, and kings
       e) Ruling through the church
 III. The Proper Might (vv. 4-5, 8*a*)

Lesson
 IV. The Proper Mystery (vv. 6-7)
   A. The Excitement About the Kingdom (v. 6)
   B. The Secret About the Kingdom (v. 7)
 V. The Proper Mission (v. 8*b-c*)
   A. The Proclaimers of the Message (v. 8*b*)
   B. The Proclamation of the Message (v. 8*c*)
 VI. The Proper Motive (vv. 9-11)
   A. The Response of Motivation
   B. The Reason for Motivation

Introduction

In the book of Acts, Luke talks about what the church is commissioned to do and how it is to be done. And in Acts 1:1–2:13, he talks about how Christ prepares the church for service.

Review

I. THE PROPER MESSAGE (vv. 1-2; see pp. 10-13)

"The former treatise have I made, O Theophilus, of all that Jesus began both to do and teach, until the day in which he was taken up, after he, through the Holy Spirit, had given commandments unto the apostles whom he had chosen."

II. THE PROPER MANIFESTATION (v. 3)

"To whom also he showed himself alive after his passion by many infallible proofs, being seen by them forty days, and speaking of the things pertaining to the kingdom of God."

A. Christ Increased the Apostles' Faith (v. 3*a*; see pp. 13-14)

B. Christ Increased the Apostles' Knowledge (v. 3*b*)

When Christ reappeared to the disciples, He taught them the same things He did before His death—"things pertaining to the kingdom of God." Therefore it's important to know what we can about the kingdom.

1. The universal kingdom of God

God rules the entire universe. Psalm 145 says, "I will extol thee, my God, O king, and I will bless thy name forever and ever. . . . Thy kingdom is an everlasting kingdom" (vv. 1, 13). He reigns even over hell. Matthew 10:28 says this about God: "Fear him who is able to destroy both soul and body in hell."

2. The mediatorial kingdom of God

A mediator is a go-between for two parties. God's rule is carried out through various people who rule for Him. Through the ages, God has carried out His mediatorial rule in different ways.

a) Ruling through man's conscience

When God created Adam, He gave him dominion over the earth (Gen. 1:26). God ruled the earth through Adam. When He wanted something done, He spoke through Adam, who carried out the command. But when Adam decided to rebel against God, he no longer mediated God's rule. God no longer had someone to rule for Him on the earth. Because of Adam's sin, the human race was cut off from God.

Between the time of the Fall and the Flood, there are only two times when God intervened with mankind: when He threw Cain out of His presence (Gen. 4:9-16) and when He brought Enoch into His presence (Gen. 5:24). Otherwise, God's rule on earth was hindered by the sinfulness of men. Genesis 6:11 says that the earth was corrupt and filled with violence.

During that era, God communicated to man through his conscience. But it's easy to ignore the conscience. It's also possible to improperly educate the conscience. The conscience can become insensitive when abused over a long period of time. Because man refused to let God rule through his conscience, God chose another method of mediatorial rule.

b) Ruling through human government

God ruled mankind through human government in the period between the Flood and the construction of the Tower of Babel. God allowed men to organize governments, and the basic law was capital punishment, which God instituted as a way to deal with criminals. Genesis 9:6 says, "Whoso sheddeth man's blood, by man shall his blood be shed; for in the image of God made he man." God developed human government and gave it the right of capital punishment to restrain people from murdering each other.

The establishment of government has still maintained itself up to today, and to an extent, God still mediates His rule through it. Romans 13:1 says, "Let every soul be subject unto the higher powers. For there is no power but of God; the powers that be are ordained of God." Yet as we will see later, God's mediatorial kingdom rule is not primarily through the government.

Is God for a One-World Government?

God has never wanted a one-world government; only when Christ establishes His millennial kingdom will God allow that. According to Genesis 11, men wanted to have a one-world government and build a tower that reached up into heaven. But God didn't want that, and He confounded the people by making them speak different languages. That scattered everyone, and the Tower of Babel was never finished. The best man can do now in his quest for worldwide cooperation is to get delegates from different countries to listen to each other through interpreters at the United Nations.

If there were a one-world government, there would be no system of checks and balances to prevent corruption. Absolute power corrupts absolutely, so it's safer to have national governments that will keep an eye on one another. Through a one-world government, it would be possible to try to wipe out Christianity. That's why Satan will attempt to form one during the Tribulation. Yet it will fall apart (Rev. 17-18) and be destroyed at the second coming of Christ (Rev. 19:19-20). The only one-world government that will survive will be the coming millennial kingdom of Christ.

c) Ruling through the patriarchs

From the time of Abraham to Moses, God's rule on earth was mediated through the patriarchs. Because Abraham was God's ruling representative on earth, he was as much a king as Saul and David were. Abraham, Isaac, Jacob, Joseph, and the other fathers of ancient Israel were the vice-regents in God's kingdom on earth.

d) Ruling through the judges, prophets, and kings

From the time of Moses to Christ, God's rule was mediated through men such as Gideon, Samuel, and David. Regardless of whether the men were judges, prophets, or kings, God ruled through them all. Some of the prophets were even greater instruments of God's rule than many of the kings! At the close of that period, God sent Jesus Christ. He was rejected, crucified, and then rose again. While He was on earth He preached a simple message: "Repent; for the kingdom of heaven is at hand" (Matt. 4:17). Whose kingdom was He talking about? His own. Christ will return someday to reign on earth as King of kings and Lord of lords. He will fulfill Isaiah 9:6, which says, "Unto us a child is born, unto us a son is given, and the government shall be upon his shoulder."

e) Ruling through the church

Between the mediatorial eras of the prophets and kings of Israel and Christ's future kingdom is a gap known as the church age. We live in that age, and it's through the church that God is now ruling. Specifically the Holy Spirit is working through the lives of all believers. If you're a Christian and you are living according to God's will, He is ruling through you. The holiness within us is what helps restrain the influence of evil in the world.

So when Christ spoke to the apostles about the things pertaining to the kingdom, He was teaching them about God's rule in the universe and on the earth. The aspect He probably focused on most was the future kingdom He will establish at His second coming. That would reassure the apostles that Jesus indeed was King. Their hopes were dashed when He died on Calvary, but when He rose again and taught about His future reign, their hopes were restored.

III. THE PROPER MIGHT (vv. 4-5, 8*a*; see pp. 15-18)

"[Christ] being assembled together with [the apostles], commanded them that they should not depart from Jerusalem, but
wait for the promise of the Father, which, saith he, ye have
heard from me. For John truly baptized with water; but ye
shall be baptized with the Holy Spirit not many days from
now. . . . But ye shall receive power, after the Holy Spirit is
come upon you."

Lesson

IV. THE PROPER MYSTERY (vv. 6-7)

A. The Excitement About the Kingdom (v. 6)

"When they [the apostles], therefore, were come together,
they asked of him, saying, Lord, wilt thou at this time re-
store again the kingdom to Israel?"

When Christ taught the apostles about the kingdom after
His resurrection, they got excited because they thought
perhaps now He would begin His reign. Old Testament
prophecy gave no indication that there would be a long period of time between the first and second comings of
Christ. The apostles were probably familiar with Ezekiel 36
and Joel 2, which say that the kingdom will come when the
Holy Spirit is poured out. When they heard Christ say the
Holy Spirit would come soon (v. 5), they thought He was
about to set up His kingdom on earth. They saw that to be
the next logical step after the atonement.

B. The Secret About the Kingdom (v. 7)

"[Christ] said unto them, It is not for you to know the
times or the seasons, which the Father hath put in his own
power."

God didn't want the disciples to know when the kingdom was coming. Can you imagine what would happen if we knew the time of the second coming? Generation after generation of Christians would probably become slack in their commitment to doing God's work. There's no need for us to know when Christ will return. Probably the only thing Christ didn't explain to the disciples about the kingdom is when it would come. Otherwise they had complete knowledge about it.

An Indirect Answer to an Incorrect Belief

Some people call themselves covenant theologians; most of them believe there is no future, literal kingdom for Israel (a view known as amillennialism). But when Jesus answered the disciples' question about the time of the kingdom's coming, He didn't tell them there would be no kingdom. He simply said that the *time* of the kingdom's coming was not for them to know. If there were no literal kingdom planned for the future, Christ would have said so in Acts 1:7.

The only thing the disciples understood about the kingdom in relation to time was that it was future. When Christ said they would soon be baptized with the Holy Spirit (Acts 1:5) the disciples thought that meant the kingdom was coming soon. But later on they understood that the time of the kingdom is unknown. Both Peter and John said Christ will come suddenly and unexpectedly (2 Pet. 3:10; Rev. 3:3).

Today, we still don't know the time of the Lord's coming. Yet there seems to be a general anticipation by many that it will be soon. I know of one man who thought Christ was going to come before January 1 of a particular year, so he sold everything he had to buy Bibles and other things to give to people. But Christ didn't come, and now the man has nothing. The Lord doesn't want us to act foolishly. In Luke 19:13 He says, "Occupy till I come." We are to keep busy with our responsibilities and not concern ourselves with the time of Christ's return. Deuteronomy 29:29 says, "The secret things belong unto the Lord our God." In 1 Thessalonians 5:1-2 Paul says, "Of the times and the seasons, brethren, ye have no need that I write unto you. For yourselves know perfectly that the day of the Lord so cometh as a thief in the night." Don't speculate about the time of the second coming.

V. THE PROPER MISSION (v. 8b-c)

A. The Proclaimers of the Message (v. 8b)

"Ye shall be witnesses unto me."

Jesus didn't say we will be theologians; He said we will be witnesses. We don't have to become master theologians capable of teaching complex doctrines before we can talk about Christ. We're simply to be witnesses: people who see something and tell others about it.

The Criteria for Being a Witness

An incident took place in my life that illustrates what a witness is: I once saw two big men beating up someone on the street. It looked like they were trying to kill him. They had broken all his ribs and kicked his face to a point beyond recognition. I heard the commotion while I was in my father's church, and I went outside where I saw people on the sidewalk watching but not helping. At first I thought it was a fight, and I told the men to break it up. But once I saw how serious the situation was, I tried to stop the assailants. They hit me, so I had the church secretary call the police. Eventually I had to go to court as an eyewitness, and I was asked to explain three things: what I saw, what I heard, and what I felt. In 1 John 1 the apostle John uses the same criteria in his witness about Christ: "That which . . . we have heard, which we have seen with our eyes, which we have looked upon, and our hands have handled . . . declare we unto you" (vv. 1, 3). A Christian witness declares to others his experience with Christ.

The Greek word translated "witnesses" in Acts 1:8 is *martures*. In the early church so many Christians died for their faith that the Greek word meaning "witness" came to mean "martyr." That's how willing the early Christians were to be witnesses for Christ. Most Christians today aren't willing to put their lives on the line, much less live in total commitment to Christ. Do you know what it means to be a living sacrifice (Rom. 12:1)? Hosea spoke of sacrifice when he said, "Take away all iniquity, and receive us graciously, that we may present the fruit of our lips" (14:2, NASB*). God asked Abraham to give up what was most precious to him by telling him to offer his son Isaac as a sacrifice (Gen. 22:1-13). The promise of a great nation through Isaac would vanish if he were killed. But Abraham was willing to obey God. That's what being a living sacrifice is about: God doesn't necessarily want you to die for Him, but He wants you to be willing to live for Him as if nothing else mattered. Peter was a witness; he talked to others about the Lord (2 Pet. 1:16). You are a witness, and you have the same mission. Are you telling others about Christ as you should?

B. The Proclamation of the Message (v. 8c)

"Both in Jerusalem, and in all Judaea, and in Samaria, and unto the uttermost part of the earth."

Christ told the apostles they were witnesses, and that they were to start their mission in Jerusalem. From there, they were to witness about Him in Judaea, Samaria, and the uttermost parts of the earth. They fulfilled the Lord's desire in about thirty years. They didn't have any sophisticated organizational plans; they just went out and did it. From the Day of Pentecost on, the early church witnessed fearlessly. They turned the world upside down (Acts 17:6). Yet many Christians today who have access to the same power the early church had aren't accomplishing as much. It takes commitment.

VI. THE PROPER MOTIVE (vv. 9-11)

"When [Christ] had spoken these things, while they beheld, he was taken up, and a cloud received him out of their sight. And while they looked steadfastly toward heaven as he went up, behold, two men stood by them in white apparel; who also said, Ye men of Galilee, why stand ye gazing up into heaven? This same Jesus, who is taken up from you into heaven, shall so come in like manner as ye have seen him go into heaven."

New American Standard Bible.

A. The Response of Motivation

Motivation is what drives you to do something. On the old "Our Gang" series, I remember one episode where the kids couldn't get a goat to pull a cart. One little boy got the bright idea of tying a carrot onto a bamboo rod and dangling it six inches in front of the goat. The boy understood the importance of motivation!

The disciples were bewildered as they watched Christ ascend to heaven. Two angels appeared and said, "Ye men of Galilee, why stand ye gazing up into heaven?" (v. 11). The disciples acted as if they were going to lose Jesus. But the angels said no; Christ was going to return. They said, "This same Jesus, who is taken up from you into heaven, shall so come in like manner as ye have seen him go into heaven" (v. 11). Knowing that would stir the disciples to greater service.

The same Christ who ascended into heaven in Acts 1:9 will return the same way. He won't be different. He will return in the same glorified body that the disciples saw when Christ joined them for breakfast by the Sea of Galilee (John 21:4-14). He will be in the same body Thomas saw when he said, "My Lord and my God" (John 20:28).

When my father was in seminary, he was young and brash. One night he went to a service featuring a preacher who called himself Father Divine and who claimed to be the Son of God. Just as the service ended and everyone was about to leave, my father stood up in the back, put his arms across the door, and said to the preacher, "Before anyone leaves, I want to ask a question. If you're really the Son of God, can you show me the nail prints in your hands?" The church became quiet, and my father was thrown out. Obviously the preacher was a false christ. He wasn't the same One who ascended into heaven in Acts 1:9, for Christ will return just the same as He left.

B. The Reason for Motivation

Knowing that Christ will return someday should motivate us to serve Him diligently. The apostle Paul said, "We labor that, whether present or absent, we may be accepted of him" (2 Cor. 5:9). Someday we will all appear before the judgment seat of Christ to receive rewards for what we did while on earth (2 Cor. 5:10). Christ said, "Behold, I come quickly, and my reward is with me, to give every man according as his work shall be" (Rev. 22:12). One of the greatest motivators for serving Jesus is that He will reward us for what we have done.

Some people think it's materialistic to look forward to those rewards, but it's not. We should look forward to the crowns we will receive. Paul did (2 Tim. 4:8). If a man loves a woman and says to her, "I love you; I want to marry you," she doesn't say to him, "You're so materialistic! It's not enough to love me; you want to have me." Marriage is the natural reward of love. Likewise, if a general wins a battle, we don't say he's selfish. A person doesn't run a race just to stop in the middle of it. You run to win. Paul said, "I, therefore, so run, not as uncertainly; so fight I, not as one that beateth the air" (1 Cor. 9:26). Paul ran so that he might obtain the prize (Phil. 3:14). Should we do any less for the Lord?

Jesus is coming with rewards for His own. When He comes, what will you have to show Him? My grandfather wrote this in his Bible: "When I stand at the judgment seat of Christ and He shows me His plan for me—the plan of my life as it might have been—and I see how I blocked Him here and checked Him there and would not yield my will, will there be grief in my Savior's eyes—grief though He loves me still? He would have me rich, but I stand here poor, stripped of all but His grace while memory runs like a haunted thing down a path I can't retrace. Then my desolate heart will well nigh break with tears I cannot shed. I will cover my face with my empty hands; I will bow my uncrowned head."

Focusing on the Facts

1. What are the different ways God has ruled His mediatorial kingdom, and how is He carrying out that rule now (see pp. 23-25)?

2. When Christ rose again and taught His disciples about the kingdom, what aspect of God's rule did He most likely focus on? Why (see p. 25)?
3. Why did the apostles get excited when Christ taught them about His kingdom after His resurrection (Acts 1:6; see p. 26)?
4. How did Christ respond to the disciples' excitement (Acts 1:7; see p. 26)?
5. What are we to do as we wait for Christ to return (Luke 19:13; see p. 27)?
6. What is a witness? What Bible passage backs up that definition (see p. 28)?
7. What happened to the Greek word meaning "witness" as a result of the many Christians who were killed in the early days of the church? What is being a living sacrifice all about (see pp. 28-29)?
8. How effective were the apostles as witnesses for Christ (see p. 29)?
9. What did the angels say to the apostles (Acts 1:11)? What was the effect of their statement (see p. 30)?
10. What announcement does Christ make in Revelation 22:12 (see p. 31)?
11. One of the greatest _____ for serving Jesus is the fact that He will return with _____ for us (see p. 31).
12. Is it materialistic to look forward to the rewards Christ will bestow when He returns? What was Paul's attitude (see p. 31)?

Pondering the Principles

1. Christ says that we are witnesses for Him. That simply means we are to tell others about Him. Read 1 John 1:3-4. What two reasons did John give for witnessing about Christ? Have you ever considered those as reasons for speaking Christ to your unsaved neighbors and friends? Read Acts 2:37-41. What kind of results were the apostles getting from their witnessing? Think about why you share the gospel with others and what kind of responses you are getting. While you do that, ask God to help you have the right motives for witnessing and to be the kind of witness that helps people see their need for Christ.

2. Some Christians go to one extreme or the other regarding the second coming: they either neglect their daily responsibilities in

anticipation of the future or they live without serious commitment to the Lord, as if Christ would never return. Consequently both groups live as poor witnesses for Christ. Based on what you learned in this lesson, what would you tell someone who neglects his present responsibilities because he's preoccupied with the second coming? What would you say to a Christian who lives without serious commitment to Christ?

3
Resources for Finishing
Our Lord's Unfinished Work—Part 3

Outline

Introduction

Review
I. The Proper Message (vv. 1-2)
II. The Proper Manifestation (v. 3)
III. The Proper Might (vv. 4-5, 8a)
IV. The Proper Mystery (vv. 6-7)
V. The Proper Mission (v. 8b-c)
VI. The Proper Motive (vv. 9-11)

Lesson
VII. The Proper Men (vv. 12-26)
    A. The Submission of the Disciples (vv. 12-15)
        1. The walk (v. 12)
            a) The description
            b) The distance
        2. The wait (vv. 13-14)
            a) The place (v. 13a)
            b) The people (vv. 13b-14)
                (1) The attendees
                (2) The action
        3. The speech (v. 15)
    B. The Suicide of a Disciple (vv. 16-20)
        1. The speech regarding prophecy (v. 16)
        2. The situation regarding Judas (vv. 17-20)
            a) The partnership of the impostor (v. 17)
            b) The plight of the impostor (vv. 18-19)
            c) The prophecy about the impostor (v. 20)

Introduction

In Acts 1:12-26 the focus is mainly on two different disciples: Judas and Matthias. There's a great contrast between the two because Matthias was a true disciple, and Judas was not. This historical narrative in the passage contains some rich truths applicable to our lives.

Review

In Acts 1 Jesus is preparing the apostles for what is about to happen in Acts 2—the birth of the church. He tells them that the Holy Spirit will descend on them and give them the power to be witnesses for Him. In Acts 1 we see what Christ did to prepare the apostles. In Acts 1:1-11 we've seen six things that helped make the apostles ready.

I. THE PROPER MESSAGE (vv. 1-2; see pp. 10-13)

II. THE PROPER MANIFESTATION (v. 3; see pp. 13-14, 22-25)

III. THE PROPER MIGHT (vv. 4-5, 8a; see pp. 15-18)

IV. THE PROPER MYSTERY (vv. 6-7; see pp. 26-27)

V. THE PROPER MISSION (v. 8b-c; see pp. 28-29)

VI. THE PROPER MOTIVE (vv. 9-11; see pp. 29-31)

Lesson

VII. THE PROPER MEN (vv. 12-26)

In Acts 1:12-26 Christ concerns Himself with replacing Judas with the proper man to carry on His work. That's consistent with the way God works: He doesn't stay detached from men but accomplishes His will through them. God is sovereign, but His plans work themselves out through the unpredictable concurrence of many human wills—some yielding and some rebellious. When Gideon was to defeat a foe, the slogan of the battle was "The sword of the Lord, and of Gideon" (Judg. 7:18). That's because the Lord was working through Gideon. When God divided the Red Sea to allow the Israelites to travel across it, He used an east wind to divide the sea and a man named Moses to lead the people (Ex. 14:21). God gives man the responsibility to carry out His will, and the selection of a new disciple to replace Judas in Acts 1 fits that pattern.

Was It Wrong for Peter to Replace an Apostle?

Some people think Matthias was chosen by Peter and that he had no business replacing Judas. However, I believe Jesus chose Matthias as a part of His plan for the birth of the church. In John 15:16 Jesus says to His disciples, "Ye have not chosen me, but I have chosen you, and ordained you, that ye should go and bring forth fruit." Now Paul was an apostle, too, even though he wasn't one of the twelve. Like the others, he was chosen by Christ (Acts 9). After Paul became converted, he spent three years in Arabia in preparation for his ministry as an apostle (Gal. 1:17-18). Luke 6:13 confirms that Christ chose the first twelve disciples; he didn't just ask them to join Him. That's what happened to Paul as well.

Acts 10 gives further confirmation about the Lord's selection. Peter said, "We are witnesses of all things which [Christ] did, both in the land of the Jews and in Jerusalem; whom they slew and hanged on a tree. Him God raised up the third day, and showed him openly; not to all the people, but *unto witnesses chosen before by God, even to us*, who did eat and drink with him after he rose from the dead. And he commanded us to preach unto the people, and to testify that it is he who was ordained by God to be the Judge of living and dead" (vv. 39-42; emphasis added). The apostles were chosen by

37

God. Not only did the Lord appoint the twelve, but he also appointed the seventy men who were sent to evangelize in Luke 10. He said, "The harvest truly is plenteous, but the laborers are few. Pray ye, therefore, the Lord of the harvest, that he will send forth laborers into his harvest" (Matt. 9:37-38). Christian service is a matter of divine appointment. God does the sending. In Romans 10:15 Paul says, "How shall they preach, except they be sent?"

There are many people today who claim to be ministers of God yet they weren't sent by Him. King Uzziah tried to usurp a ministry he was not ordained for and was inflicted with leprosy as a result (2 Chron. 26:16-21). Unless God has called you by putting a burden on your heart (cf. 1 Tim. 3:1), don't enter into the ministry. James wrote, "Let every man be swift to hear, slow to speak" (1:19). He also said, "Be not many teachers, knowing that we shall receive the greater judgment" (3:1). Be available if God's calling you into the ministry, but don't do something you haven't been called to do.

Other Scripture verses confirm the fact that God appoints the leaders of His people. Ephesians 4:11-12 says that God "gave some, apostles; and some, prophets; and some, evangelists; and some, pastors and teachers; for the perfecting of the saints for the work of the ministry." The Greek word translated "gave" conveys the idea that God appointed those men their roles. First Corinthians 12:28 says, "God hath set some in the church: first apostles, second prophets, third teachers."

Although some say Peter chose Matthias on his own, God actually chose Matthias. The Old Testament prophesied that Judas would be replaced (Ps. 109:8), so the change was a part of God's plan.

A. The Submission of the Disciples (vv. 12-15)

In Luke 24:49 Jesus tells the disciples to stay in Jerusalem until the Holy Spirit arrives: "Tarry ye in the city of Jerusalem, until ye be endued with power from on high." In Acts 1 He tells them not to depart from Jerusalem but to "wait for the promise of the Father . . . ye shall be baptized with the Holy Spirit not many days from now" (vv. 4-5). It was important for the disciples to wait because the Holy Spirit couldn't come until Christ was back in heaven (John 16:7). It is the Holy Spirit who would give the disciples the power to be witnesses to the world.

1. The walk (v. 12)

   "Then returned [the disciples] unto Jerusalem from the mount called Olivet, which is from Jerusalem a sabbath day's journey."

   The disciples were obedient to the Lord's request; they were submissive. That's a trait we all need to seek.

   a) The description

   The Mount of Olives is lovely. It's a small mountain that rises about four hundred feet above the bottom of the Kidron Valley, just to the east of Jerusalem. Since Jerusalem is only about two hundred feet above the Kidron Valley, that means you can look down over Jerusalem from the top of the Mount of Olives. Going down the backside of the Mount of Olives, you would eventually arrive in Bethany, and beyond that, Jericho and the Dead Sea. Luke 24:50 tells us that when Christ ascended, it was from the side of the Mount of Olives facing Bethany. So that's where the disciples began their journey back to Jerusalem.

   b) The distance

   Acts 1:12 says the disciples' trip to Jerusalem was "a sabbath day's journey," which was two thousand cubits (about three thousand feet or a little more than half a mile).

   The idea of traveling only two thousand cubits on the Sabbath day was not an ordinance of the Old Testament. Bible scholar C. I. Scofield commented that "this measure may have been determined by the distance that the children of Israel were required to allow between themselves and the ark of the covenant at the passage of the Jordan (Josh. 3:4); for the rabbis may have assumed that the same limit prevailed between the tents of the people and the tabernacle—a distance that the Israelites would need to walk in order to worship" (*The New Scofield Reference Bible* [New York: Oxford, 1967], p. 1206). Consequently the term "sabbath day's journey" became synonymous with the distance of two thousand cubits. Acts 1:12 wasn't saying that the disciples were going to Jerusalem on the Sabbath day but that they went two thousand cubits.

By traveling two thousand cubits from the backside of the Mount of Olives, they would have ended up just inside the east gate of Jerusalem.

2. The wait (vv. 13-14)

a) The place (v. 13a)

"When they were come in, they went up into an upper room."

The disciples most likely gathered in the same upper room where the Last Supper was held and where Jesus appeared to them after His resurrection. In those days, houses frequently had upper rooms or chambers. The upper rooms were like living rooms. It was a place for fellowship or devotions. In Acts 9 we read that a dead widow named Dorcas was placed in an upper room prior to her planned burial (she was resurrected by Peter). The upper room the disciples went to must have been large because it could accommodate 120 people (Acts 1:15). It may have belonged to a wealthy homeowner.

While the disciples were waiting for the Holy Spirit, they didn't just stay in the upper room. Luke 24:53 says they "were continually in the temple, praising and blessing God." So the upper room served as a meeting place.

b) The people (vv. 13b-14)

"Where abode Peter, and James, and John, and Andrew, Philip, and Thomas, Bartholomew, and Matthew, James, the son of Alphaeus, and Simon the Zealot, and Judas, the son of James. These all continued with one accord in prayer and supplication, with the women, and Mary, the mother of Jesus, and with his brethren."

(1) The attendees

> Judas the son of James is not to be confused with Judas Iscariot. The latter had already committed suicide after betraying the Lord. Eleven of the disciples were there along with "the women, and Mary, the mother of Jesus, and with his brethren" (v. 14). "The women" were probably the ladies who were with Jesus throughout His ministry, death, and resurrection: Mary Magdalene, Mary the wife of Clopas, Mary and Martha, Salome, and perhaps others (cf. Luke 8:1-3).

> Christ's mother and half-brothers were also in the upper room. (James, Joseph, Simon, and Jude—whom we see mentioned in Matthew 13:55—were half-brothers because they were direct descendants of their father, Joseph, yet Jesus was conceived by the Holy Spirit.) James and Jude both wrote epistles in the New Testament. According to John 7:5 Christ's brothers at one time weren't believers, but they had become believers by the time Acts 1 was written. I'm sure it was exciting for Christ to know His brothers were believers. How did they become saved? Scripture doesn't say, but I think it may have happened when James saw Christ after the resurrection (1 Cor. 15:4, 7).

As the Mother of Christ, Does Mary Have a Special Status?

It's important to note that in Scripture Mary herself is never exalted; she is exalted only in relation to the child she bore. In Mark 3 Christ Himself indicates that she has no supernatural status. As He was teaching in a house, His brothers and mother came calling for Him. The people listening to Him said, "Behold, thy mother and thy brethren outside seek for thee" (v. 32). Verses 33-35 say, "He answered them, saying, Who is my mother, or my brethren? And he looked round about on those who sat about him, and said, Be-

41

hold my mother and my brethren! For whosoever shall do the will of God, the same is my brother, and my sister, and mother." Jesus' mother and brothers needed redemption just like anyone else; they weren't above sin because of their relationship to Christ. (In fact, Scripture says that Mary brought a sin offering to the Temple [Luke 2:24; cf. Lev. 12:1].)

Acts 1:14 says that the disciples were praying *with* Mary, not *to* her. For centuries the Roman Catholic church has taught that Mary is our co-redemptrix—that both she and Christ redeemed mankind, and that we need to pray to her to get Christ to listen to us. But that's not taught in the New Testament. Mary certainly is blessed. She may have been one of the loveliest women who ever lived and a wonderful wife and mother. But it's wrong to elevate her to the status of divinity. Mary was kneeling in prayer to her son, just like everyone else. No candles were being burned to her. She is never mentioned again in the New Testament. Paul never talks about her when he discusses the doctrines relating to redemption. A great disservice is done by those who say we need to go through Mary to reach God or Christ. Does that mean Catholics aren't Christians? Not necessarily. I believe there are Christians within the Catholic church, but they sometimes have to circumvent Catholic theology to get to the truth of God's Word.

Where Did the Worship of Mary Come From?

If the teaching about Mary's co-redemptrix status didn't come from the New Testament, how did it originate? A look back into history reveals the answer. (The discussion that follows comes from Alexander Hislop's *The Two Babylons* [Neptune, N.J.: Loizeaux, 1959.)

In Genesis 10:10 we read about the beginning of a kingdom called Babel (later known as Babylon). Its founder was a hunter named Nimrod (Gen. 10:8-9). Nimrod was the grandson of Ham and the great-grandson of Noah. He was the apostate of the patriarchal age; he was the one who started false worship. The first idolatrous object of man's worship was the Tower of Babel. The false religion at Babel spawned a number of complex, strange, mysterious religions. Many are still in existence in some form today.

Nimrod had a wife named Semiramis I. Because Nimrod founded the Babylonian mystery religions, his wife became the high priestess of those religions. Babel was the fountainhead of all false religions, and when false religions abound again during the end times, they are referred to as Babylon (Rev. 17-18).

The activity going on in Babel upset God. He scattered the people so they would stop building the tower (Gen. 11:7-8). Consequently the Babylonian mystery religions spread throughout the world. They became known by different names in different countries, but they had the same origin. Semiramis herself was the object of much false worship. In Assyria and Nineveh she was known as Ishtar, in Phoenicia she was Ashteroth, in Egypt she was Isis, in Greece she was Aphrodite, and in Rome she was Venus.

Religious writings about Semiramis say she was impregnated by a sunbeam and gave birth to a son named Tammuz. Semiramis was considered a perpetual virgin, and her son virgin born. Later on, a wild boar killed Tammuz, and Semiramis went into mourning for forty days. After those days of weeping and praying, Tammuz supposedly rose from the dead. Every year Tammuz was believed to die and retreat to the shadows of the netherworld. Only the laments of those who adored him could bring him back to the land of the living. That shows us the origin of Lent: it comes from the pagan practice of forty days of weeping and self-denial for the resurrection of Tammuz. Lent has no connection whatsoever with Christ or the Bible.

The mother-child cult formed by the stories about Semiramis and Tammuz are the basis for various false religions. In Phoenicia Tammuz was known as Baal, in Egypt he was known as Osiris, in Greece he was known as Eros, and in Rome he was known as Cupid. The mother and child are known by different names, but they are still the same characters. When paganism began infiltrating Christianity during the fourth century, misguided worshipers substituted Mary and Jesus for the pagan figures in the mother-child cult they were accustomed to.

There are several parallels between the worship of Semiramis and the teachings of Roman Catholicism: Semiramis was called the Queen of Heaven (as is Mary), her forty days of mourning parallels Lent, the Babylonian mystery religions had priests administering parallel sacramentals, they dedicated virgins to their gods—that's where the idea of the convent originated—and they believed in purgatory. These facts are not included as a criticism of the people in the Roman Catholic church but of the doctrines of the church.

Let's expand on one of the parallels above: both Semiramis and Mary are considered the queen of heaven. In Jeremiah 44 we read about disobedient Jews who fled to Egypt. Verses 15-17 say, "All the men who knew that their wives had burned incense unto other gods, and all the women who stood by, a great multitude, even all the people who dwelt in the land of Egypt, in Pathros, answered Jeremiah, saying, As for the word that thou hast spoken unto us in the name of the Lord, we will not hearken unto thee. But we will certainly do whatsoever thing goeth forth out of our own mouth, to burn incense unto the queen of heaven, and to pour out drink offerings unto her, as we have done, we, and our fathers, our kings, and our princes." Where did such worship originate? Egyptian idolatry.

In Ezekiel 8 the prophet Ezekiel is unhappy about the idols in the Temple. In verses 13-14 he states specifically that women were in the Temple weeping for Tammuz, the son of Semiramis. The worship of Semiramis in Jeremiah 44 and her son Tammuz in Ezekiel 8 are idolatrous practices that have been carried over into Christianity.

There is no reason to think Mary should be elevated above other women. We shouldn't pray to her; she can't answer our prayers. In Acts 1:14 we read that she was praying to Christ along with everyone else in the upper room. No one was praying to her. Mary needed to pray to the Lord just as much as anyone else.

(2) The action

Acts 1:14 tells us that all the people in the upper room were "with one accord in prayer and supplication." They were gathered together for fellowship and prayer. One thing they weren't praying for was the coming of the Holy Spirit. The Spirit's coming didn't depend on their prayers. Acts 1:4 says that the Holy Spirit was a promise of the Father. They already had the promise; it was just a matter of waiting. In fact when the Spirit did come in Acts 2:2, the people weren't even in prayer.

Everyone was praying (Acts 1:14) because it was the first time they had been removed from Jesus.

44

The only way they could communicate to Him from that point onward was through prayer. They were entering a new age; no one had ever prayed to Jesus before. So Acts 1:14 cannot be said to indicate that one must ask for the Holy Spirit's presence in his life. The baptism of the Spirit has nothing to do with your prayers; it is a sovereign act of God that occurs at the moment of salvation (Rom. 8:9; 1 Cor. 12:13).

The overarching principle at this point in the disciples' lives is not so much that they spent time rejoicing at the Temple and praying in the upper room but that they were obedient to Christ's command to stay in Jerusalem until the Holy Spirit came.

3. The speech (v. 15)

"In those days Peter stood up in the midst of the disciples, and said (the number of names together was about an hundred and twenty)."

We now see Peter getting ready to talk about replacing Judas with another disciple. The phrase "in those days" refers to the ten-day period between Christ's ascension and the Spirit's coming.

The number of people in the upper room was 120. There were probably about 500 more believers in Galilee, but at Jerusalem that may have been all there were. Can you imagine starting a worldwide movement with only 120 people? It's even more astounding when you realize that they weren't superhuman. They were people just like us. The odds were overwhelming. But their small number was more than compensated for by the power they derived from God. Within thirty years the gospel spread all over the known world and penetrated Rome. For example, Paul's first letter to the Thessalonians was written shortly after he left them, and he was already able to commend the Thessalonian church for spreading their faith far abroad (1 Thess. 1:8). They were witnesses energized by the Holy Spirit. When you're obedient to God, He will work in amazing ways through your ministry.

B. The Suicide of a Disciple (vv. 16-20)

At this time, the disciples were all probably wondering why Judas betrayed Jesus. Christ had told them that one day the disciples would sit on twelve thrones (Matt. 19:28), but now there were only eleven disciples. So the things Peter says are a message from God that Judas's betrayal was expected, and that the prophecy in Matthew 19:28 wasn't wrong.

1. The speech regarding prophecy (v. 16)

"Men and brethren, this scripture must needs have been fulfilled, which the Holy Spirit, by the mouth of David, spoke before concerning Judas, who was guide to them that took Jesus."

The Holy Spirit was using Peter to tell the disciples that what Judas did was prophesied in the Old Testament. Within that verse we see a definition of inspiration: it's when the Holy Spirit uses the mouth of a speaker or the pen of a writer.

Peter reassured them that God's plan wasn't thwarted because Judas betrayed Jesus. God doesn't lose those who really belong to Him. Jesus says in John 17:12, "Those that [the Father] gavest me I have kept, and none of them is lost, but the son of perdition, that the scripture might be fulfilled." Judas's betrayal fulfilled Scripture. That doesn't mean God made Judas betray Jesus; it simply means that He used Judas's actions to accomplish His purpose. God can work through men whether they are saved or not. God used an evil high priest named Caiaphas to state a prophecy about Christ (John 11:51).

What Scripture verses did Judas's betrayal fulfill? Peter brings that up in verse 20, which we'll examine soon.

2. The situation regarding Judas (vv. 17-20)

a) The partnership of the impostor (v. 17)

"For he was numbered with us, and had obtained part in this ministry."

Judas was called to be a disciple by divine appointment, but that doesn't mean he was saved. John 6:64 says, "Jesus knew from the beginning who they were that believed not, and who should betray him." Later in verse 70 He says to His disciples, "Have not I chosen you twelve, and one of you is a devil?" Verse 71 says, "He spoke of Judas Iscariot, the son of Simon; for he it was that should betray him, being one of the twelve." Christ knew Judas would never believe. In fact, Judas stayed with Christ for money only; he was the treasurer of the group (John 12:6). His greed is evident in John 12:1-8, where he gets angry because a woman anointed Jesus' feet with a costly ointment. He said the ointment could have been sold and the money given to the poor. But the real reason for his anger was that any money that went into the treasury became available to him (v. 6). Judas was hungry for money up to the end. He sold Jesus for thirty pieces of silver (believed to be thirty tetradrachmas). A drachma was the Greek equivalent to the Roman denarius, the average day's wage, and is valued at sixteen cents. That means Judas betrayed Christ for approximately twenty dollars or 120 days' wages.

The Sad Truth About Judas

The most tragic aspect of the story of Judas is that he could have received Christ. The Lord gently warned him again and again, but Judas never repented. When I graduated from seminary I wrote my thesis on Judas Iscariot. I became more and more saddened as I read all I could about him. He lived in Christ's light for three years, yet his life ended horribly. Judas stands out for all time as the classic apostate. He had the greatest opportunity of anyone to receive Christ, and he turned it down. He was among the disciples, but he never was really one of them. When he betrayed Jesus, it didn't foul up God's plan; instead, it fulfilled prophecy. God knew what would happen, and Judas's betrayal led up to Christ's crucifixion.

Matthew 27 tells us what happened after Judas betrayed Jesus: "When he saw that [Jesus] was condemned, [he] repented, and brought again the thirty pieces of silver to the chief priests and elders, saying, I have sinned in that I have betrayed innocent blood" (vv. 3-4). Verse 3 says he repented, but it wasn't a repentance that led to salvation (cf. 2 Cor. 7:10). He felt guilty because he realized he had betrayed an innocent man. He knew Jesus was not a criminal. At least he had enough moral fortitude to be convinced of that.

When Judas confessed to the Jewish religious leaders his wrongdoing and tried to return the thirty pieces of silver, they said, "What is that to us?" (v. 4). They didn't care that Jesus was innocent. They got what they wanted. Verse 5 says Judas "cast down the pieces of silver in the temple, and departed, and went and hanged himself." Jesus said, "Woe unto that man by whom the Son of man is betrayed! It had been good for that man if he had not been born" (Matt. 26:24).

Verses 6-8 say, "The chief priests took the silver pieces, and said, It is not lawful to put them into the treasury, because it is the price of blood. And they took counsel, and bought with them the potter's field, to bury strangers in. Wherefore, that field was called, The field of blood, unto this day." The hypocrisy of the religious leaders is shocking: they had just paid Judas to help them condemn an innocent man, but they were careful to observe that the money couldn't go back into the Temple treasury.

b) The plight of the impostor (vv. 18-19)

"Now this man purchased a field with the reward of iniquity; and falling headlong, he burst asunder in the midst, and all his bowels gushed out. And it was known unto all the dwellers at Jerusalem, insomuch as that field is called in their proper tongue, Akeldama, that is to say, The field of blood."

The money Judas returned was used to purchase the field he happened to die in. According to Matthew 27:5 he hung himself, but apparently the rope broke and he fell. Evidently he tried to hang himself on one of the rocky parapets that were around that field, which is somewhere between the Valley of Hinnom and the Valley of Kidron.

Writings from the early church reveal the hatred people had for Judas. Late first-century church Father Papias said Judas became so swollen from disease that he couldn't get through places where chariots could pass. Another writer said his eyes were so swollen that they could not see the light, and that the rest of his body was covered with worms (cited in *The Ante-Nicene Fathers: Translations of the Writings of the Fathers down to A.D. 325*, vol. 1 [Grand Rapids: Eerdmans, 1973 reprint], p. 153). Statements like those are false and totally unnecessary. We should have a sense of sorrow for the opportunity Judas wasted. It's sad to see someone close to the truth and walk away from it. Hebrews 10:29 says, "Of how much sorer punishment, suppose ye, shall he be thought worthy, who hath trodden under foot the Son of God, and hath counted the blood of the covenant, with which he was sanctified, an unholy thing."

c) The prophecy about the impostor (v. 20)

"It is written in the book of Psalms, Let his habitation be desolate, and let no man dwell therein; and his bishopric let another take."

The first part of verse 20 was prophesied in Psalm 69:25. To say the habitation of Judas would be desolate is the same as saying he would be removed— that he would drop out. The second part of verse 20 comes from Psalm 109:8, which says Judas's office or position would be filled by someone else. Judas was replaced not with someone like him but with another whose heart was right. By quoting those two psalms, Peter reassured his fellow disciples that Judas's departure fulfilled prophecy. It wasn't an accident that circumvented God's plan.

C. The Selection of the Next Disciple (vv. 21-26)

In the next few verses we read about the qualifications for an apostle.

1. The criteria (vv. 21-25)

"Wherefore of these men who have companied with us all the time that the Lord Jesus went in and out among us, beginning from the baptism of John unto that same day that he was taken up from us, must one be ordained to be a witness with us of his resurrection. And they appointed two, Joseph, called Barsabbas, who was surnamed Justus, and Matthias. And they prayed, and said, Thou, Lord, who knowest the hearts of all men, show which of these two thou hast chosen, that he may take part in this ministry and apostleship, from which Judas by transgression fell, that he might go to his own place."

There were three requirements the new apostle had to meet: first, he had to have been with the other disciples and Jesus from the baptism of John to the ascension; second, he had to be a witness of Christ's resurrection; and third, he had to be chosen by God.

Was Paul Really an Apostle?

Paul was an apostle, but he was an apostle of a different era. To affirm that, he described himself as an apostle chosen by God at the beginning of most of his epistles. He met two of the requirements stated in Acts 1:21-25: he was a witness of the resurrected Christ on the road to Damascus (Acts 9:1-8), and he was chosen by God to be a witness for Him (Acts 22:14-15).

Two men were chosen from the group in the upper room as candidates for the position vacated by Judas: Matthias and Joseph (also known as Barsabbas). This is the only place in the New Testament where those men are mentioned. The new apostle wasn't necessarily destined to be a prominent minister. Often it's the quiet, behind-the-scenes people who accomplish a lot for God's kingdom.

Acts 1:24 says the people in the upper room prayed. That's because they knew the new apostle had to be chosen by God. Only the Lord knew which was the right man, and the other people wanted God to reveal which one it was. The Lord chose the first eleven disciples, and they knew He would choose the twelfth also.

Why was Judas replaced by a new apostle? Acts 1:25 says it was so the new apostle would "take part in this ministry and apostleship, from which Judas by transgression fell, that he [Judas] might go to his own place." That's a shocking statement; Peter was saying Judas belonged in hell. That's where Judas chose to go because he rejected Christ. As Jesus said, Judas was "the son of perdition" (John 17:12). When a person dies, his eternal destiny is crystallized. Every person has a place in eternity reserved for him depending on what he does with Jesus Christ. Judas rejected Him and went to hell.

2. The choice (v. 26)

"They gave forth their lots; and the lot fell upon Matthias, and he was numbered with the eleven apostles."

God chose Matthias to become the new disciple. Notice that Joseph didn't become upset. He didn't demand the lots to be cast again or walk out angrily. I wonder how he felt about not being chosen. However he felt, I'm sure he stayed with the disciples and continued on in the Lord's work. We don't know why God chose Matthias, but it should be enough to know that if God did the choosing, He made the right choice. It's not right to question those whom the Lord calls as ministers. First Timothy 5:19 says we are never to bring an accusation against an elder or overseer unless there are two or three witnesses. We are never to speak badly of God's ministers, even though we might disagree with them. To do so is to walk on tenuous ground. First Samuel 26:23 says not to act against the Lord's anointed.

Was It Wrong for the Men to Draw Lots?

How did the apostles know God chose Matthias? The men drew lots. Some people say that's a form of gambling and that they shouldn't have drawn lots. But in the Old Testament God used such methods to manifest His will in a physical way (e.g., 1 Sam. 14:37-42). Sometimes God would talk directly out of heaven, sometimes He spoke through prophets, and sometimes He would communicate through the Urim and Thummin stored in the breastplate of the high priest. But Acts 1:26 is the last time in Scripture you see God working through lots. From the New Testament age onward —from the time God's people became indwelt with the Holy Spirit in Acts 2—God has chosen to reveal His will by the leading of the Holy Spirit within us. Notice that the apostles prayed before the lots were chosen. They knew God would show His choice through the selection of lots. That's confirmed in Proverbs 16:33, which says, "The lot is cast into the lap, but the whole disposing thereof is of the Lord." God was in full control of the choosing in Acts 1:21-26.

Conclusion

The two primary lessons we learn from Acts 1:12-26 are these: God chooses those who serve Him, and every man's destiny is determined by what he does with Christ. Matthias became an apostle because God chose him, and Judas went to hell because he rejected Christ. For Christians, the message is to live in prayerful submission to God at all times. And for non-Christians, the message is that your eternal destiny is based on whether you receive or reject Christ. If you receive Christ, you'll go to the Father's house in heaven; but if you reject Christ, you'll go to hell.

Focusing on the Facts

1. What does Christ concern Himself with in Acts 1:12-26 (see p. 37)?
2. Some people think Peter was out of line in choosing Matthias. Is that true? Explain (see pp. 37-38).
3. What does Christ tell the disciples to do in Luke 24:49, and why (see p. 38)?
4. How did the disciples respond to the Lord's request (Acts 1:12; see p. 39)?
5. What did the disciples do while in the upper room (Luke 24:53; see p. 40)?
6. As Christ's mother, is Mary any more special than other people? How can we tell based on Christ's own words and on what happened in the upper room (see pp. 41-42)?
7. What do some people believe the disciples were praying for (Acts 1:14)? What's the real reason they were praying (see pp. 44-45)?
8. The Holy Spirit uses Peter to tell the disciples what in Acts 1:16 (see p. 46)?
9. Does the fact that Judas was called to be a disciple mean he was saved? Explain (see p. 47).
10. What kind of repentance did Judas sense after he betrayed Christ (2 Cor. 7:10; see p. 48)?
11. What Scripture verses did Judas fulfill in his betrayal (see pp. 49-50)?
12. What were the three requirements the new apostle had to meet (see p. 50)?
13. Was there anything wrong with drawing lots to determine who would be the next apostle? Explain (see p. 52).
14. What are the two primary lessons in Acts 1:12-26 (see p. 52)?

Pondering the Principles

1. Jesus told the disciples to wait in Jerusalem until the promised Holy Spirit came upon them (Luke 24:49). The disciples submitted to the Lord's command; they returned to Jerusalem and waited ten days for the Holy Spirit to come. Sure enough, He came as promised (Acts 2). When the Lord makes a promise, He will keep it. Sometimes we don't know how He will fulfill His promises, but we should never lose trust. Psalm 119:89-90 en-

courages us with this truth: "Forever, O Lord, thy word is settled in heaven. Thy faithfulness is unto all generations." What are some ways God has shown His faithfulness to you? Let Him know you're grateful for what He's done.

2. Judas was condemned to hell because he rejected Christ. After he died, there was nothing he could do to change his eternal destiny. Occasionally when you share the gospel with people, you may meet someone who is postponing the decision to receive Christ because he thinks he can do it later. The best way to respond to such a person is to point out that no one knows the moment of his death. Hebrews 9:27 says, "It is appointed unto men once to die, but after this the judgment." Once a person dies, it's too late to change his eternal destiny. That's why it's important to receive Christ now. Memorize Hebrews 9:27 to help you explain what happens to a person after death and the consequences of postponing a decision for Christ.

4
The Baptism of the Holy Spirit—Part 1

Outline

Introduction
A. Identifying the Transition
B. Illustrating the Transition

Lesson
I. The Evidence of the Spirit's Coming (vv. 1-4)
   A. The Specifics of the Spirit's Arrival (v. 1)
      1. The reason for the Spirit's coming
         a) The Spirit's coming didn't depend on men
         b) The Spirit's coming was timed to fulfill prophecy
            (1) Two types of prophecy
            (2) Three fulfilled prophecies
               (a) The feast of Passover
               (b) The feast of firstfruits
               (c) The feast of harvest
      2. The location of the Spirit's coming
   B. The Signs of the Spirit's Arrival (vv. 2-4)
      1. The wind (v. 2)
         a) The suddenness of the phenomena
         b) The source of the phenomena
      2. The fire (v. 3)
         a) The evidence of the baptism
         b) The extent of the baptism
         c) The explanation about the baptism
         d) The examination of the cloven tongues
      3. The tongues (v. 4)
         a) The distinction of the filling
         b) The duration of the filling
         c) The display of the filling

Introduction

A. Identifying the Transition

In Acts 1 Christ prepares the way for the birth of the church, and in chapter 2 the church is born. In Acts 1 the disciples are waiting for the Holy Spirit, and in Acts 2 He comes. In chapter 1 they are equipped by Christ, and in chapter 2 they are empowered by the Spirit. First they are told to wait, then they are sent forth. In Acts 2 we see the fulfillment of Acts 1:8: "Ye shall receive power, after the Holy Spirit is come upon you; and ye shall be witnesses unto me."

In Acts 2 is one of the greatest transitions recorded in Scripture. It marks the end of the old age and the beginning of the new. Up to now, the Spirit was with God's people, but from now on He would indwell them. In the Old Testament era, men served God out of love along with a fear of the consequences of breaking God's law. But from now on, they would serve God out of love for Christ with the energy of the indwelling Holy Spirit. All believers have the Spirit within them and are in an invisible union with each other and Christ. Paul referred to the church as a mystery because it was not revealed in the Old Testament (Eph. 3:3-6), but in Acts 2 we see that mystery unfolding. In the Old Testament God revealed Himself to man through the law and the sacrificial system, but with Christ God revealed Himself in a redemptive manner. Christ died, was buried, rose again, and ascended to heaven. Then the Holy Spirit was sent to dwell in men.

It's difficult to communicate the significance of that transition; only God can define the change that took place. John 7:37-39 defines it this way: "In the last day, that great day of the feast, Jesus stood and cried out, saying, If any man thirst, let him come unto me, and drink. He that believeth on me, as the scripture hath said, out of his heart shall flow rivers of living water. (But this spoke he of the Spirit, whom they that believe on him should receive; for the Holy Spirit was not yet given, because Jesus was not yet glorified)." In God's redemptive plan, the age of the Holy Spirit couldn't begin until Jesus ascended and was glorified in heaven. In Acts 1 the disciples see Christ ascend into heaven, and in Acts 2 the promised Spirit comes. This is a new dispensation—a whole new age.

B. Illustrating the Transition

What is the church? The Greek word translated "church" (*ekklēsia*) means "called-out ones." In Ephesians 5:22-29 the church is seen as Christ's bride. John 15:1-10 describes it as the branches on a vine, the vine being Christ. The church is also seen as a flock (John 10), a household (Gal. 6:10), adopted children (Rom. 8:15-17), and a building or temple with Christ as its foundation (Eph. 2:20-22). Most descriptively, it is a body (1 Cor. 12:12-27). Just as the human body is made up of parts that function together, so is the church a body of individuals brought together in union with Christ through the Holy Spirit. We all work together as a whole.

Christ was manifest in a physical body when He came to earth; now He is manifest in a multiplicity of people who form a spiritual body. We are a fellowship knit together with Christ as the head (Eph. 5:23). We are dependent on each other, just as the parts of the human body are. All barriers are abolished. Paul said that in Christ "there is neither Jew nor Greek, there is neither bond nor free, there is neither male nor female; for ye are all one" (Gal. 3:28). Everyone who is a Christian is indwelt by Christ, and that's what makes up the church. The church isn't the building; it's the people—those who know Christ by faith.

Do All Christians Have the Holy Spirit?

Some people say not all Christians have the Holy Spirit. But the Bible clearly says that all Christians are a body of believers indwelt by the Spirit (1 Cor. 12:13). Romans 8:9 says, "If any man have not the Spirit of Christ, he is none of his." He is the source of instruction, power, comfort, and security. Christ promised the disciples they would receive the Spirit, and that's exactly what happened in Acts 2. Since then, all believers have received the Spirit at the moment of conversion.

Lesson

I. THE EVIDENCE OF THE SPIRIT'S COMING (vv. 1-4)

As we look through Acts 2, keep in mind that we're looking at the birth of the church. It's at this time that Christ's promise of the baptism of the Holy Spirit (Acts 1:5) and the indwelling of the Spirit (Acts 1:8) take effect. Later we'll see how both occur simultaneously at the time of salvation. The only reason both didn't happen the moment the disciples were saved during Christ's lifetime is that Christ had not then ascended into heaven (John 7:39). Acts 2 presents a unique situation. It cannot be used to say that a believer is baptized with the Spirit some time after salvation. The Spirit came to baptize and indwell the disciples in Acts 2 because that's when God planned for the Spirit to come. There had to be a beginning somewhere.

A. The Specifics of the Spirit's Arrival (v. 1)

"When the day of Pentecost was fully come, they were all with one accord in one place."

1. The reason for the Spirit's coming

    a) The Spirit's coming didn't depend on men

    The Day of Pentecost came ten days after Christ's ascension. The disciples were still together. The Spirit came, yet nowhere in Acts 2 do we read that He arrived as a result of the disciples' prayers or fulfillment of some special spiritual requirements. The Spirit came on this day because that's when God planned for Him to come. He didn't send the Spirit in response to anyone's spiritual activity.

    b) The Spirit's coming was timed to fulfill prophecy

    The proper interpretation of Acts 2:1-4 depends on understanding what Pentecost was all about. The Greek word for "pentecost" means "fiftieth day." The Jews had a feast called the feast of Pentecost because it took place fifty days after the feast of firstfruits, which followed the Passover. The same feast was also called the feast of harvest (Ex. 23:16) and the feast of weeks (Ex. 34:22).

The feast of Pentecost celebrated the wheat harvest. It also commemorated the giving of the Mosaic law, because the Jewish people believe the law was given to them about fifty days after the beginning of their journey to the Promised Land. The Exodus began when God sent an angel to slay all the firstborn of Egypt. After the Israelites left Egypt, it became traditional to celebrate God's giving of the law alongside the feast of harvest. The Jews still do that today. As we'll see in a moment, it was no accident that the Holy Spirit came on the Day of Pentecost.

(1) Two types of prophecy

There are two kinds of prophecies: verbal prophecies, which tell what will happen in the future, and typical prophecies, which picture something that will happen in the future. An example of verbal prophecy is Isaiah 7:14, where we read, "Behold, the virgin shall conceive, and bear a son, and shall call his name Immanuel" (cf. Matt. 1:22-23). A typical prophecy is the Passover lamb, which is a picture of Christ, who was the final Passover Lamb (1 Cor. 5:7). Although the typical prophecies may not be as obvious or direct as the verbal prophecies, that doesn't make them any less important. They also have to be fulfilled.

(2) Three fulfilled prophecies

The Spirit's coming on the Day of Pentecost fulfilled a typical prophecy. There are three feasts mentioned in Leviticus 23 that I'd like us to look at, and the last one will relate to the Day of Pentecost.

(a) The feast of Passover

The first mentioned is the Passover (Lev. 23:4-5). To escape the plague on the firstborn in Egypt, the Israelites had to kill a lamb and put its blood on the doorposts and lintel. The angel of death then passed over those houses. Christ's blood fulfills the typical prophecy of the Passover lamb, for His death protects us from God's wrath. And according to God's plan, Christ died on Passover. First Corinthians 5:7 calls Christ our Passover. So not only was the Passover lamb in Exodus 12 a picture of Christ, but it was also an indication that Christ would die on Passover—the fourteenth of Nisan, which corresponds to a day in late March or early April.

(b) The feast of firstfruits

This feast was on the day after the Sabbath following the Passover—the Sunday after Passover (Lev. 23:9-14). The firstfruits were taken from barley crops. A farmer who wanted to determine if he would have a good crop that year would go to different sections of the barley field and pull out some samples. If they all looked good, he could say that the whole crop was guaranteed to be good based on the firstfruits. By doing this they would be reminded to praise God for the upcoming harvest. It was a good reminder to trust in God.

The feast of firstfruits is a picture of the resurrection of Christ. In John 12:24 Jesus says of Himself, "Except a grain of wheat fall into the ground and die, it abideth alone; but if it die, it bringeth forth much fruit." In 1 Corinthians 15:20 Paul says, "Now is Christ risen from the dead and become the first fruits of them that slept." Just as the feast of firstfruits showed that the rest of the harvest would be good, so Christ's resurrection shows we will also be resurrected. Jesus says in John 14:19, "Because I live, ye shall live also."

(c) The feast of harvest

Fifty days after the feast of firstfruits came the feast of harvest (Lev. 23:15-16). It is also known as Pentecost. The wheat was not ready to be harvested at the time of this feast; nevertheless, two loaves were made. The idea of the feast was to celebrate the completion of harvest in advance. The feast of harvest predicts what happened on the Day of Pentecost in Acts 2. Christ died on the Passover, rose on the feast of firstfruits, and made possible the enjoyment of those events on Pentecost.

Matthew 13:30 says that when Christ returns He will take in the harvest and separate the wheat (believers) from the tares (unbelievers). What guarantees that Christians will be in that wheat harvest? Second Corinthians 5:5 says that all believers have "the earnest of the Spirit." Ephesians 1:13-14 says, "After ye believed, ye were sealed with that Holy Spirit of promise, who is the earnest of our inheritance." The Greek word translated "earnest" (*arrabōn*) can mean "pledge," "engagement ring," or "guarantee." The Spirit of God within you is the guarantee of your inheritance in heaven. Because God has given you His Spirit, He will never withhold anything from you. The Spirit came to indwell the disciples on Pentecost, fulfilling the typical prophecy of the feast of harvest.

Notice that the wheat gathered on the feast of harvest was made into loaves. That pictures the descent of the Holy Spirit on the Day of Pentecost. It was the Spirit who brought the separate disciples together to make one Body, the church. Christ's church is not a loosely gathered group of people but a group that has been blended into one common Body. We know that the loaves represent the church because they contained leaven (Lev. 23:17). The barley on the feast of firstfruits didn't have leaven because it represented Christ. Leaven represents sin, and Christ is sinless.

The Holy Spirit came on the Day of Pentecost to fulfill typical prophecy. Some people believe that the baptism of the Holy Spirit is given only to believers who ask for it. That reveals a misunderstanding of why the Holy Spirit came. It overlooks the fulfillment of a typical prophecy in Leviticus 23. Jesus died, rose, and sent the Spirit all at the right moments—the times God ordained beforehand. The Spirit's coming on the Day of Pentecost was not an accident; it was a promised event.

2. The location of the Spirit's coming

Acts 2:1 says that when the Spirit came, the disciples "were all with one accord in one place." Where was this place? The next verse says they were in a house. Some commentators think that refers to the Temple, which is the house of the Lord. But if Luke meant the Temple, he probably would have said so. In Acts 2:46 he talks about people who were "with one accord in the temple." Why would Luke use a different word when he talks about the same situation? Since he used the Greek word for house (*oikos*), they were most likely in a house. I also think the 120 people mentioned in Acts 1:15 were there, not just the 12 disciples. Otherwise that would have left 108 people out of the baptism of the Spirit, which at this time was to signal the birth of the church.

B. The Signs of the Spirit's Arrival (vv. 2-4)

1. The wind (v. 2)

"Suddenly there came a sound from heaven like a rushing mighty wind, and it filled all the house where they were sitting."

a) The suddenness of the phenomena

The church was born suddenly; it came into being instantaneously. The people in the house probably weren't expecting a sound from heaven (notice it was a sound *like* a wind and not a wind itself). At the rapture, the church will leave just as quickly. Jesus says in Revelation 22:12, "Behold, I come quickly." He will return to take His church from the earth in an instant. God has the sovereign right to determine when the church begins and ends; its beginning and ending have nothing to do with anyone's prayers.

b) The source of the phenomena

The sound like a wind came from heaven. The source was God, not man or Satan. It was not a real wind but a sound like wind. In Scripture, wind is often an emblem of the Holy Spirit. John 3:8 says, "The wind bloweth where it willeth, and thou hearest the sound of it, but canst not tell from where it cometh, and where it goeth; so is every one that is born of the Spirit." Generally the Greek word translated "spirit" is *pneuma*, which also means "breath" or "wind." But in Acts 2:2 the Greek word is *pnoēs*, which means "a blast of breath." It's not a gentle breeze; it's more like a strong gust.

What fantastic phenomena those people were witnessing: there was no motion in the air, but it sounded as if a hurricane came raging out of heaven! It happened suddenly and was as if the very breath of God had reached the earth. The people in the house were all baptized with the Holy Spirit. They were completely enveloped by the breath of God. Later on we read that unbelievers came to the scene. They were curious about the sound they had heard and came to the house to see what was happening.

Is the Baptism of the Spirit an Experiential Event?

Today people define the baptism of the Spirit as an experience. But in Acts 2:2 the baptism was nonexperiential. The people were merely sitting in the room, became baptized, and showed no reaction at that moment. Baptism with the Spirit is a sovereign act of God. A good example of this can be found in what happened when you became a Christian. The moment you received Christ you were justified. Did you suddenly think, *Oh, there goes justification!* No, justification is a judicial, nonexperiential reality. It is the state of being adopted into God's family on the basis of your faith in Christ.

Some people point to the speaking in tongues in Acts 2:4 as the experiential reaction to the baptism with the Spirit. But, as we'll see when we get to verse 4, that was a result of the filling of the Spirit. If a person does have an experience, it will be from the filling of the Spirit, not the baptism.

Defining the Baptism of the Spirit

Throughout the New Testament are verses that clarify the baptism of the Spirit.

1. 1 Corinthians 12:12-13

Paul said, "As the body [the church] is one, and hath many members, and all the members of that one body, being many, are one body, so also is Christ. By one Spirit were we all baptized into one body, whether we be Jews or Greeks, whether we be bond or free; and have been all made to drink into one Spirit." The baptism of the Holy Spirit is when God's Holy Spirit takes a believer and places him in the Body of Christ. You don't shout or feel goose bumps when that happens; it's a divine transaction.

2. Galatians 3:27

Further definition appears here: "As many of you as have been baptized into Christ have put on Christ." Paul didn't say that the baptism results in an experiential response; rather it establishes our union with Christ and His church. When you put your faith in Christ, you instantaneously become one with Him and all fellow believers.

3. 1 Corinthians 6:17

"He that is joined unto the Lord is one spirit." As a Christian, you are one with Christ through the Spirit.

4. Galatians 2:20

Paul wrote, "I am crucified with Christ: nevertheless I live; yet not I, but Christ liveth in me; and the life which I now live in the flesh I live by the faith of the Son of God." How do all the believers in the church become one with each other and Christ? By the baptism of the Spirit.

5. Romans 6:3-4

"Know ye not that, as many of us as were baptized into Jesus Christ were baptized into his death? Therefore, we are buried with him by baptism into death, that as Christ was raised up from the dead by the glory of the Father, even so we also should walk in newness of life." Paul wasn't talking about water baptism but our baptism into Christ. When you become a Christian you are immersed in Christ and become one with Him.

6. Colossians 2:9-12

Here we read that in Christ "dwelleth all the fullness of the Godhead bodily. And ye are complete in him . . . in whom also ye are circumcised with the circumcision made without hands, in putting off the body of the sins of the flesh by the circumcision of Christ; buried with him in baptism, in which also ye are risen with him through the faith of the operation of God." Our union with Christ is spiritual: when we're saved we're buried with Christ in His death and rise with Him in His resurrection.

7. 1 Peter 3:20-21

Peter talked of the Flood as a typical prophecy of baptism with the Spirit in verse 20. Verse 21 says, "The like figure unto which even baptism doth also now save us (not the putting away of the filth of the flesh, but the answer of a good conscience toward God)." Peter was speaking of the baptism that saves us, Spirit baptism—not water baptism.

8. Ephesians 2:22

Believers "are built together for an habitation of God through the Spirit." The Holy Spirit filled a physical house in Acts 2, and in the same moment He filled a spiritual house composed of believers at the birth of the church.

9. John 17:11, 21-23

If the baptism of the Spirit didn't make all believers one, then Jesus' prayer in John 17 remains unanswered. In verses 11, 21-23, He prays to the Father that His followers would be one. The baptism of the Spirit made that possible; He has made us one inwardly and outwardly. Sometimes there will be disunity when we allow sin in our lives. But we are one Body. We are mutually dependent on each other in the ministry of our spiritual gifts. By recognizing the baptism of the Spirit as the event that brings us into oneness, we realize that that is how Jesus' prayer in John 17 was answered.

2. The fire (v. 3)

"And there appeared unto them cloven tongues as of fire, and it sat upon each of them."

a) The evidence of the baptism

The cloven tongues that sat on their heads weren't actually fire; they appeared to be like fire. These parted tongues appeared over each one, a testimony that each without exception had received the Holy Spirit. They were visible proof that the Spirit came.

b) The extent of the baptism

Two things happen when you're baptized with the Spirit: you are baptized into one body, and the Spirit is put in you (1 Cor. 12:13). So the cloven tongues in Acts 2:3 show not only that the Spirit had come but also that every believer received the Spirit internally. And when the Spirit comes to dwell within you, He will stay there forever (John 14:16).

c) The explanation about the baptism

Some people believe the cloven tongues really were fire—the baptism with fire talked about in Matthew

3:11. In that verse John the Baptist says, "I, indeed, baptize you with water unto repentance, but he who cometh after me is mightier than I, whose shoes I am not worthy to bear; he shall baptize you with the Holy Spirit, and with fire." However, verse 12 defines the baptism with fire by saying that someday Jesus will "thoroughly purge his floor, and gather his wheat into the granary, but he will burn up the chaff with unquenchable fire." Matthew 3:11 talks about the fire of eternal judgment. John the Baptist was saying that either you're baptized with the Holy Spirit (eternal security) or with fire (eternal judgment).

d) The examination of the cloven tongues

We don't know exactly what the cloven tongues of fire were. All we do know is that they appeared on every believer, hovering overhead like little parted flames. They were a visible manifestation of the Spirit's arrival. The people weren't attuned enough spiritually to comprehend the momentous arrival of the Spirit apart from a visible manifestation. A similar situation took place when Jesus was baptized by John the Baptist (Matt. 3:16). The Holy Spirit descended upon Jesus like a dove.

Can a Christian Lose the Holy Spirit?

Some people wonder if Christians who have fallen into sin can still have the Holy Spirit in them. In 1 Corinthians 3:16 Paul rebukes some sinning Christians by saying, "Know ye not that ye are the temple of God, and that the Spirit of God dwelleth in you?" Paul didn't say, "You have now lost the Holy Spirit." He told them they needed to get rid of the sin in their lives. Possession of the Spirit is the mark of a Christian (Rom. 8:9).

3. The tongues (v. 4)

"And they were all filled with the Holy Spirit, and began to speak with other tongues, as the Spirit gave them utterance."

a) The distinction of the filling

Now that the people had been placed in union with Christ and each other, God filled them with His Spirit; then they began speaking in tongues. The filling didn't happen until *after* the baptism. Speaking in tongues didn't come as a result of the baptism. The filling of the Spirit and the baptism of the Spirit are two distinct things. At the birth of the church the Holy Spirit came first to baptize everyone into the Body of Christ. Then He filled them so they could be a powerful testimony. Scripture commands us to be filled with the Spirit (Eph. 5:18) but never tells us to seek the baptism of the Spirit. There's no need to, because it happens when you receive Christ.

When you become a Christian, you will receive both the baptism and the filling of the Spirit. From then on it's a matter of being repeatedly filled with the Spirit, which means yielding to Him.

b) The duration of the filling

In Ephesians 5:18 Paul says, "Be filled with the Spirit." That command is in the present tense and could literally be translated, "Be being continuously filled with the Spirit." That means that unlike the baptism of the Spirit, it's a continuous activity, not a one-time event. Remember the joy you experienced when you came to Christ? You sensed the blessing and love of God and probably wanted to tell others of Christ even though you didn't know what to say. That feeling comes from the filling of the Spirit. As you continuously yield your life to the Spirit, He will continue to fill you. But if there's sin in your life, He can't fill you. Two things can't occupy the same space at the same time.

c) The display of the filling

As you keep yielding to the Spirit, you'll see results in your life. Some of the results of being filled with the Spirit include "speaking to yourselves in psalms and hymns and spiritual songs, singing and making melody in your heart to the Lord, giving thanks always for all things unto God and the Father in the name of our Lord Jesus Christ" (Eph. 5:19-20). Other results include husbands loving their wives and wives submitting to their husbands, children obeying their parents, masters treating their servants properly, and servants doing an honest day's work (Eph. 5:21–6:9). So the filling of the Spirit has an immediate response and happens repeatedly. That is confirmed elsewhere in the book of Acts.

(1) Acts 4:8—Peter was filled with the Holy Spirit when he preached about Christ to the "rulers of the people, and elders of Israel."

(2) Acts 4:31—After some people in the early church prayed, "the place was shaken where they were assembled together; and they were all filled with the Holy Spirit, and they spoke the word of God with boldness."

(3) Acts 6:5, 8—Some men needed to be chosen for a particular ministry in the early church, and Stephen was one of the chosen ones (v. 5). He was a man filled with the Holy Spirit. As a result of that filling, he was full of faith and power (v. 8).

(4) Acts 7:55-60—On one occasion when Stephen was filled with the Spirit he preached such a powerful sermon that unbelievers stoned him to death.

(5) Acts 9:17, 20—After Paul's conversion Ananias came to him and said, "Jesus . . . hath sent me, that thou mightest receive thy sight, and be filled with the Holy Spirit" (v. 17). In verse 20 we see Paul immediately preaching about Christ in the synagogues.

(6) Acts 11:22-24—The church at Jerusalem sent Barnabas out to preach to people as far away as Antioch. He exhorted people, telling them to cling to the Lord. Why did he do that? Because he was "a righteous man, and full of the Holy Spirit" (v. 24).

(7) Acts 13:9-11—Paul, when he was filled with the Holy Spirit, rebuked a sorcerer.

(8) Acts 13:52–14:1—When the disciples were filled with joy and the Holy Spirit, they went into a synagogue in Iconium and preached the gospel.

The filling of the Spirit is what enables us to do the job God wants us to do or be the person He wants us to be. It's not the same as the baptism of the Spirit. As long as you're yielding control of your life to the Spirit, you will be filled by the Spirit. Baptism grants you the power of the Spirit, and the filling turns it on. To yield your life to the Spirit means to have no sin in your life. Everything you want to do should be in line with God's will, not your own.

When the Day of Pentecost came, the disciples and other believers were gathered together. God's sovereign plan ordained that to be the day the Spirit would come, initiating the birth of the church. When the sound like a mighty wind was heard, everyone in the room was baptized into the Body of Christ. They became one, just as Jesus asked in John 17. To make sure everyone present knew they had received the Spirit, cloven tongues like fire appeared over their heads. Having been baptized in the Spirit and possessing Him within, they were all filled with the Spirit. Then they spoke in tongues (a subject we will explore in the next lesson). Their lives were already in submission to God at the time. And when they were filled, they became a powerful testimony for God.

Focusing on the Facts

1. Describe some of the incidents we read about in Acts 1 and their counterparts in Acts 2 (see p. 56).
2. How does God define the change that took place in Acts 2 (John 7:37-39; see p. 56)?
3. What is the church? What are some of the scriptural metaphors for the church (see p. 57)?
4. How do Ephesians 5:23 and Galatians 3:28 describe the church (see p. 57)?

5. Do all Christians have the Holy Spirit? Support your answer with Scripture (see p. 57).
6. Explain how the coming of the Spirit on the Day of Pentecost fulfills the typical prophecy of the feast of harvest (see pp. 61-62).
7. In what way was the church born, and how will it leave the earth (see pp. 62-63)?
8. Acts 2:2 says a sound like a violent wind was heard in the room. What was the source of the sound? In Scripture, what does wind sometimes symbolize (see p. 63)?
9. What definition does Paul give of the baptism of the Holy Spirit in 1 Corinthians 12:12-13? What do other Scripture verses teach about the baptism of the Spirit (see pp. 64-66)?
10. What were the evidence and the extent of the baptism of the Spirit (see p. 66)?
11. Does Matthew 3:11 have anything to do with the baptism of the Spirit seen in Acts 2:3? Explain (see pp. 66-67).
12. Why did the disciples need a visible manifestation of the baptism (see p. 67)?
13. Can a Christian lose the Holy Spirit? Explain (see p. 67).
14. What is the distinction between the baptism and the filling of the Spirit (see p. 68)?
15. Explain the significance of the command in Ephesians 5:18 being in the present tense (see p. 68).
16. What are some of the results of being filled with the Spirit (see pp. 68-69)?
17. As long as you're _____ control of your life to the _____, you will be filled by the Spirit (see p. 70).

Pondering the Principles

1. To learn more about the Holy Spirit, read John 14:16-17, 26. What title does verse 16 give to the Holy Spirit? How long will the Spirit abide with us (v. 16)? What does verse 17 say about the Spirit in relation to unbelievers? What about believers? What does verse 26 say the Spirit will do for us? First Corinthians 2:10-11 confirms that the Holy Spirit is God's own Spirit. What additional things might that tell you about the Spirit?

2. Ephesians 5:19–6:9 lists the results of being filled with the Holy Spirit. Do these things characterize your life? As a way of yield-

ing more of your life to the Holy Spirit, consider what specific actions you can take now that would strengthen or bring about those characteristics in your life.

3. Reread the section entitled "Defining the Baptism of the Spirit." Using your own words, briefly write out how you would respond to someone who says the baptism of the Spirit happens some time after a person becomes saved.

5
The Baptism of the Holy Spirit—Part 2

Outline

Introduction

Review
I. The Evidence of the Spirit's Coming (vv. 1-4)
   A. The Specifics of the Spirit's Arrival (v. 1)
   B. The Signs of the Spirit's Arrival (vv. 2-4)
      1. The wind (v. 2)
      2. The fire (v. 3)

Lesson
      3. The tongues (v. 4)
         a) Explaining the phenomenon of speaking in tongues
         b) Examining the purpose of speaking in tongues
            (1) The Samaritans in Acts 8
            (2) The Gentiles in Acts 10
            (3) John the Baptist's disciples in Acts 19
         c) Evaluating the power of speaking in tongues
II. The Effect of the Spirit's Coming (vv. 5-11)
   A. The Crowd (v. 5)
   B. The Confusion (vv. 6-8)
      1. The sound that attracted them (v. 6a)
      2. The speech that amazed them (vv. 6b-8)
   C. The Communication (vv. 9-11)
      1. The languages (vv. 9-11a)
      2. The message (v. 11b)
III. The Explanation of the Spirit's Coming (vv. 12-13)
   A. The Curiosity (v. 12)
   B. The Callousness (v. 13)

Conclusion

Introduction

In the second chapter of Acts we see two great promises come to pass: the birth of the church and the coming of the Spirit. In Matthew 16:18 Christ says, "I will build my church, and the gates of hades shall not prevail against it." In John 14:16-17 the Lord says, "I will pray [to] the Father, and he shall give you another Comforter, that he may abide with you forever; even the Spirit of truth . . . ye know him; for he dwelleth with you, and shall be in you." Acts 2:1-13 chronicles the fulfillment of those two promises.

Review

I. THE EVIDENCE OF THE SPIRIT'S COMING (vv. 1-4)

    A. The Specifics of the Spirit's Arrival (v. 1; see pp. 58-62)

    B. The Signs of the Spirit's Arrival (vv. 2-4)

        1. The wind (v. 2; see pp. 62-63)

        2. The fire (v. 3; see pp. 66-67)

What Does It Mean to Be Filled with the Spirit?

Throughout the New Testament the word *filled* is used many times. It commonly refers to something that overpowers everything else. For example, Acts 6:5 says Stephen was a man filled with faith. His overwhelming belief in God carried him through the horrible stoning that led to his death in Acts 7:58-60. Luke 6:11 describes the scribes and Pharisees as being filled with anger. When a person is filled with fury, that emotion dominates all others. First Corinthians 13 and 1 John 3 teach the importance of being filled with love to the point it is preeminent in all you do.

Being filled with the Holy Spirit means you're yielding totally to the Spirit's control in your life. If you're a Christian you already have the baptism of the Spirit (1 Cor. 12:13), He lives within you (Rom. 8:9). That happened at salvation. But the filling of the Spirit

74

can come and go. Paul says in Ephesians 5:18 to always be filled with the Spirit.

Ephesians 5:19–6:9 gives the results of being filled with the Spirit. Colossians 3:16–4:1 states that the same results will happen if you "let the word of Christ dwell in you richly" (Col. 3:16). So to be filled with the Spirit you need to let the Word of Christ saturate your mind.

Lesson

3. The tongues (v. 4)

"They were all filled with the Holy Spirit, and began to speak with other tongues, as the Spirit gave them utterance."

a) Explaining the phenomenon of speaking in tongues

When the people in the room became filled with the Spirit, they began speaking in tongues, a manifestation of that reality. The Greek word translated "tongues" (*glōssa*) means "language." In verse 11 the word clearly refers to various dialects. So gibberish or ecstatic speech weren't present in Acts 2, but real languages and dialects were. Verses 9-11 specify which languages were being spoken. Notice that the languages came as a result of being filled with the Spirit. Many advocate that tongues come as a result of being baptized in the Spirit. But that's not what happened in Acts 2. Baptism in the Spirit is a nonexperiential event.

The phenomenon of speaking in tongues was a special event for that era. Just because it happened at the birth of the church doesn't mean tongues will be present each time someone is filled with the Spirit. If you look at the list of results Paul gives from being filled with the Spirit (Eph. 5:19–6:9), you'll notice that tongues—speaking in other languages—isn't included. Husbands and wives will love each other; so will parents and children. Employers and employees will have good working relations. But by the time the book of Ephesians was written, tongues were not a manifestation of the filling of the Spirit anymore.

An Inconsistent Testimony

Some of those who believe the filling of the Spirit enables them to speak in tongues don't manifest the results listed in Ephesians 5:19–6:9. They claim to speak in tongues but don't submit to their husbands, or they fail to love their wives in a sacrificial way. Some provoke their children to anger. Others are not good employers or employees. If such people really were filled with the Spirit, it would be manifest in right relationships with the significant people in their lives.

b) Examining the purpose of speaking in tongues

The miracle of speaking in tongues has a strategic purpose in Acts 2. At that time Jewish people from all over the world were in Jerusalem for the feast of Pentecost. We are told that when Titus besieged Jerusalem, an event that occurred around Passover, there were approximately three million people in the city. First-century Jewish historian Josephus also mentions that great multitudes of Jews from other nations were present in Jerusalem for the feast of Pentecost (*Wars* II.iii.1). As we'll see later, God used this speaking in other languages to help the foreign Jews hear about Him in their native languages. The purpose of tongues becomes more apparent as we look further in the book of Acts.

(1) The Samaritans in Acts 8

Verses 14-17 say, "When the apostles who were at Jerusalem heard that Samaria had received the word of God, they sent unto them Peter and John, who, when they were come down, prayed for them, that they might receive the Holy Spirit; for as yet he was fallen upon none of them; only they were baptized in the name of the Lord Jesus.

76

Then laid they their hands on them, and they received the Holy Spirit."

Peter and John went to visit a group of Samaritans. Now the Jewish people despised the Samaritans because they were descendants of Jews who had intermarried with Gentiles. In fact, the Jews wouldn't even travel through Samaria; that's how intense their hatred was.

By the time of Acts 8, the gospel message had spread from Jerusalem to Samaria. Some Samaritans were becoming Christians. The tendency of the Jewish people would have been to see the Samaritans as second-class Christians. To keep that from happening, the Holy Spirit did something special. He allowed the Samaritans to become converted without being baptized into the Body of Christ. He wanted some important Jews to be present when that happened. That way the Jews would realize the Samaritans were one with them. Peter and John were two important Jewish Christians at the time, and it wasn't until their arrival in Samaria that the Holy Spirit came. The Spirit wanted Peter and John to testify that the Samaritans were one in the Body of Christ with the Jews. I believe the Samaritans spoke in tongues when they received the baptism and filling of the Spirit; otherwise the apostles would have had no way of confirming that the Jews and Samaritans were being brought into one Body.

(2) The Gentiles in Acts 10

In Acts 10 Peter visits a Gentile named Cornelius. The gospel message was really spreading by then. Verses 44-46 say that while Peter was speaking to him and his family, "the Holy Spirit fell on all them who heard the word. And they of the circumcision who believed were astonished, as many as came with Peter, because on the Gentiles also was poured out the gift of the Holy Spirit. For they heard them speak with tongues." The

Jewish believers who were with Peter were astonished to see the Gentiles receive the Holy Spirit. In this instance, the tongues weren't for communicating so much as they were for evidence that the Gentiles were also part of the church.

In Acts 11 Peter recounts to his fellow apostles the miraculous event of Acts 10: "As I began to speak, the Holy Spirit fell on them, as on us at the beginning. Then remembered I the word of the Lord, how he said, John indeed baptized with water; but ye shall be baptized with the Holy Spirit. Forasmuch then, as God gave them the same gift as he did unto us, who believed on the Lord Jesus Christ, what was I, that I could withstand God?" (vv. 15-17). That last statement shows that there was no way to deny the Gentiles had received the Holy Spirit. Had it happened any other way, Peter might not have believed it.

When Peter told the Jerusalem council what happened to the Gentiles, some of the Pharisees raised objections. The council met together to decide if the Gentiles could really be considered a part of the church. Acts 15:6-9 says, "The apostles and elders came together to consider of this matter. And when there had been much disputing, Peter rose up, and said unto them, Men and brethren, ye know how that a good while ago God made choice among us, that the Gentiles by my mouth should hear the word of the gospel, and believe. And God, who knoweth the hearts, bore them witness, giving them the Holy Spirit, even as he did unto us; *and put no difference between us and them*" (emphasis added). The reason the Gentiles received the Holy Spirit the same way the Jews did in Acts 2 was to confirm that they, too, were part of the church. Speaking in tongues was the visible proof.

(3) John the Baptist's disciples in Acts 19

By the time we reach Acts 19 there's one other group of people that hadn't been included in the

78

Body of Christ: a little group of twelve Old Testament saints who had been baptized by John the Baptist. They didn't know Christ had risen and sent the Holy Spirit. Verses 1-4 say, "It came to pass that, while Apollos was at Corinth, Paul having passed through the upper borders came to Ephesus and, finding certain disciples, he said unto them, Have ye received the Holy Spirit since ye believed? And they said unto him, We have not so much as heard whether there is any Holy Spirit. And he said unto them, Unto what, then, were ye baptized? And they said, Unto John's baptism. Then said Paul, John verily baptized with the baptism of repentance, saying unto the people that they should believe on him who should come after him, that is, on Christ Jesus." At that point, Paul went on to speak about Christ.

Verses 5-6 continue, "When they heard this, they were baptized in the name of the Lord Jesus. And when Paul had laid his hands upon them, the Holy Spirit came on them, and they spoke with tongues, and prophesied." As with the Samaritans in Acts 8 and the Gentiles in Acts 10, the Spirit made clear to an apostolic witness that the disciples of John the Baptist were also part of the church.

Through the book of Acts you can see the marvelous genius of the Holy Spirit in putting together the Body of Christ. There is no one part of the Body that can say, "We have something you don't have." Once it was proven that Jews, Samaritans, Gentiles, and the remnant of Old Testament saints could come into the Body of Christ, there was no need for the filling of the Spirit to be accompanied by tongues-speaking. In Ephesians 2 Paul speaks of Jew and Gentile being made one in the Lord: "[Christ] is our peace, who hath made both one, and hath broken down the middle wall of partition between us" (v. 14). So everyone who became a Christian from Acts 19 onward was placed into the Body by the baptism of the Spirit without any need for external confirmation. Before that the Spirit gave the gift of speaking in tongues to the different parts of the church—in the presence of the apostles—that there might not be any question about who belonged. The unity of the Body is now secure.

What happened in the book of Acts is not a pattern for us today. It's not doctrinal teaching; it's the historical record of the transition that took place during the birth of the church. We can't say, "If you're a Samaritan, you don't get the Spirit until so many days after receiving Christ." By the time Paul wrote his epistles, doctrine regarding the Holy Spirit was clearly defined. At the point of salvation, every believer receives the Spirit and is placed into the Body by the baptism of the Spirit (1 Cor. 12:13).

c) Evaluating the power of speaking in tongues

Acts 2:4 says that the people who were filled with the Spirit on the Day of Pentecost "began to speak with other tongues, as the Spirit gave them utterance." It was the Holy Spirit who controlled the speakers. An individual who is filled with the Spirit is controlled by the Spirit.

How long does the filling of the Spirit last? As long as your life is yielded to the Holy Spirit. That's a constant discipline. However, don't let that make you worry about the future; you can yield only for the present moment anyway. You can't live in the future. Just yield in the present moment you live in, and when it's past, you can yield in what's to come. Don't think, *How can I yield my life to the Spirit for eighty years?*

Acts 2:1-4 gives the evidence of the Spirit's coming. The people in the room heard the sound like a wind, saw cloven tongues that appeared to be like fire, and spoke the different languages. There was no question that the Holy Spirit had come. The promise of Jesus came true. Every Christian today possesses the Holy Spirit. Because the Spirit dwells within us, we are able to see God work within us "exceedingly abundantly above all that we ask or think" (Eph. 3:20).

The Purpose of Miracles in the Apostolic Era

When the people in Acts 2 spoke in different languages, they were speaking of the wonderful works of God (Acts 2:11). They weren't preaching the gospel. The preaching came later on when Peter rose to speak (vv. 14-40).

God was using the different languages to get the attention of unbelieving Jews. He wanted them to realize that something supernatural was happening. Then they would know that Peter's preaching was also from a divine source. In the earliest days of the church, the apostles' preaching was always accompanied by signs, wonders, and mighty deeds. Speaking in tongues didn't substitute for preaching, nor did any of the other miracles. The miraculous events simply preceded the preaching to confirm its supernatural origin.

Second Corinthians 12:12 says, "Truly the signs of an apostle were wrought among you in all patience, in signs, and wonders, and mighty deeds." Hebrews 2:3 says, "How shall we escape, if we neglect so great salvation, which at the first began to be spoken by the Lord, and was confirmed unto us by them that heard him." How did the apostles confirm their message? Verse 4 says God bore them witness "both with signs and wonders, and with diverse miracles and gifts of the Holy Spirit." The miraculous gifts were to confirm the divine source of the apostles' message.

Can Missionaries Acquire New Languages Overnight?

If the gift of tongues is still supposed to be present in the church, as some say, then something is terribly wrong. Commentator Albert Barnes said, "The gift of miracles is withdrawn. The apostles, by that miracle, simply were empowered to speak other languages. That power must still be had if the gospel is to be preached. But it is now to be obtained, not by miracle, but by slow and careful study and toil" (*Notes on the New Testament—Acts* [Grand Rapids: Baker, 1971], p. 23).

If the gift of speaking different languages still exists, then for some strange reason God is requiring missionaries to take many years of language study so they can preach the gospel. He's making it hard to reach out to other countries. But why would God require years of intense study to fulfill the Great Commission when He could simply give the gift of languages? It would seem that if the gift still existed, that would happen. But since it doesn't, we need to study other languages. We can't make the experience in Acts 2 the norm for all Christians. It happened at a special time among certain people for a specific reason. An organization such as Wycliffe Bible Translators would be overjoyed if the gift of speaking other languages were still present, because many of its missionaries spend years laboring to translate the gospel into other languages.

II. THE EFFECT OF THE SPIRIT'S COMING (vv. 5-11)

A. The Crowd (v. 5)

"There were dwelling at Jerusalem Jews, devout men, out of every nation under heaven."

The latter half of that verse is an idiomatic statement; it means there were Jews from many other countries present in Jerusalem. Who were they? The verse says they were devout men. The Greek word translated "devout" (*eulabeis*) means "cautious." They were reverent; they came to Jerusalem for the feast of Pentecost because they didn't want to offend the Lord. Proverbs 9:10 says, "The fear of the Lord is the beginning of wisdom."

B. The Confusion (vv. 6-8)

1. The sound that attracted them (v. 6a)

"Now when this was noised abroad, the multitude came together."

What was the noise that was heard abroad? Some say it was the speaking in different languages, mentioned later in verse 6. However, the literal translation of the Greek text is, "But this sound [Gk., *phonēs*, which is singular] having come, the multitude came together." Whatever they heard, it was a single sound. The Greek verb *genomenēs* is in that statement and indicates that the sound was heard at one specific time. The only time a single sound occurred at a specific time was when the sound like a mighty wind was heard earlier in verse 2. So the crowd was drawn by that great sound.

2. The speech that amazed them (vv. 6b-8)

"[They] were confounded, because every man heard them speak in his own language. And they were all amazed and marveled, saying one to another, Behold, are not all these who speak Galileans? And how hear we every man in our own tongue, wherein we were born?"

When the crowd gathered to see what was happening, they heard the apostles and their friends speaking different languages. They were confounded—the Greek root word means "to pour together." The foreign Jews were all mixed up. They were shocked to hear the people in the room speaking in their own languages.

What amazed them even more was that the speakers were Galileans. The Jews of that time didn't have high regard for Galileans. They viewed them as uneducated people. In John 1:46 Nathanael says, "Can any good thing come out of Nazareth?" (Nazareth was one of the cities in Galilee.) When Jesus told the Jews He was a prophet from Galilee, they said, "Search, and look; for out of Galilee ariseth no prophet" (John 7:52).

The Galileans had a distinct dialect that gave away their background. Some people said they knew Peter was one of Christ's disciples because of his speech (Matt. 26:73). The Galileans who were speaking in other languages were speaking as if those languages had been their native tongue (Acts 2:8). Evidently their dialect didn't impede what was happening. The foreign Jews were dumbfounded; there was no logical explanation for it.

C. The Communication (vv. 9-11)

1. The languages (vv. 9-11a)

"Parthians, and Medes, and Elamites, and the dwellers in Mesopotamia, and in Judaea, and Cappadocia, in Pontus, and Asia, Phrygia, and Pamphylia, in Egypt, and in the parts of Libya about Cyrene, and sojourners of Rome, both Jews and proselytes, Cretans, and Arabians."

That is the roll call of languages spoken by those who were filled with the Spirit. Among the people who recognized their native languages were Jews from Asia Minor, Egypt, and Rome. There were proselytes, who were converts of Judaism. There were people from the island of Crete, as well as Arabians from the peninsula between the Red Sea and the Persian Gulf.

2. The message (v. 11b)

"We do hear them speak in our tongues the wonderful works of God."

There's no evidence that those who were speaking in tongues were proclaiming the gospel; we simply read that they declared the wonderful works of God. Why is that? Once the Spirit attracted the attention of the visiting Jews through the windlike sound and the varying languages, the foreign Jews had two choices: they could attribute the miracle to Satan or to God. Because the people speaking in tongues were praising God, that eliminated the possibility of it being a miracle of Satan.

The Holy Spirit had the people who were speaking in tongues praise God so that the foreign Jews would know God was working in their midst. Once that became obvious, Peter could get up and preach. They would know Peter's words would also be from God. What a beautiful strategy for introducing people to Christ!

What exactly does it mean to speak about the wonderful works of God? That was a Jewish custom of the time; it meant reciting from Scripture the miraculous things God had done. We see this practice evident in Exodus 15:11, where we read, "Who is like unto thee, O Lord . . . doing wonders?" In Psalm 26:6-7 David says, "I will wash mine hands in innocence . . . that I may make known with the voice of thanksgiving, and tell of all thy wondrous works." Psalm 40:5 says, "Many, O Lord, my God, are thy wonderful works which thou hast done." Psalm 77:11 says, "I will remember the works of the Lord; surely I will remember thy wonders of old." In Isaiah 25:1 we read, "O Lord, thou art my God; I will exalt thee, I will praise thy name; for thou hast done wonderful things."

Those who were speaking in tongues in Acts 2 were praising God. This was an excellent setup for Peter, who stood up in verse 14 to proclaim the gospel. Even during his sermon, Peter spoke from the Old Testament and connected all that he said with God. In verse 17 he quotes the prophet Joel and in verses 22-24 proclaims that Jesus was approved by God, delivered by God, and raised by God. In verse 30 he says Jesus was promised by God and in verse 33 that Jesus was exalted by God. Then he concluded by saying, "Therefore, let all the house of Israel know assuredly, that God hath made that same Jesus, whom ye have crucified, both Lord and Christ" (v. 36).

The Holy Spirit has a specific strategy in mind in Acts 2. The events that took place didn't happened haphazardly. The ultimate end of the baptism and filling with the Spirit and the speaking in different languages was to open the door for Peter to preach the gospel.

III. THE EXPLANATION OF THE SPIRIT'S COMING (vv. 12-13)

The crowd listening to the apostles was composed of unbelieving Jews. Later in Acts 2 we read that even with the miraculous evidence they saw, some still rejected Christ. They were the kind who say, "I've made up my mind; don't confuse me with the facts." You can give such people all kinds of evidence, but they still won't believe the truth. That proves bringing people to salvation is not just a matter of how well we argue. God's sovereignty is involved in a person's salvation, because it is the Spirit who breaks down a person's resistance to Christ. How did the crowd in Acts 2 respond?

A. The Curiosity (v. 12)

"And they were all amazed, and were perplexed, saying one to another, What meaneth this?"

The crowd didn't yet understand what was happening because the gospel hadn't been preached yet. The multitude of languages was only a sign to get them to listen. They all wanted to know what was going on.

B. The Callousness (v. 13)

"Others, mocking, said, These men are full of new wine."

This response from some members of the crowd wasn't simply a suggestion explaining what was happening; it was mockery. The Greek word translated "wine" makes clear the mockery. *Oinos* refers to strong, fermented wine. When a person has had so much of it, there's no question he is drunk. But the Greek word used here (*aleukos*) refers to sweet, freshly pressed grape juice. So the callous observers were saying, "These men are such babies that when they take a little sip of grape juice, they become drunk. Look at them!" They attributed the multiplicity of languages from Galilean speakers about the wonderful works of God to drunkenness. What blindness! To them, the events taking place were a joke. The Jewish people who thought themselves wise didn't know that God chose the foolish things of the world to confound them (1 Cor. 1:27). In John 8 Jesus says the Jewish religious leaders didn't understand Him because He spoke the truth (vv. 43, 45). They were of their father the devil (v. 44).

The mockery of Acts 2:13 was only the beginning of rejection from callous Jews. In Acts 4:7 such men question the apostles, in Acts 4:17 they threaten them, in Acts 5:18 they imprison them, in Acts 5:40 they beat them, and in Acts 7:58 they stone Stephen. The gospel either draws people to Christ or causes them to reject Him with hatred. That's seen throughout the book of Acts.

Conclusion

The Spirit of God has been given to you just as He was given to the apostles on the Day of Pentecost. He can work through you—not in the miraculous way He did in Acts 2, but in a sense that is indeed miraculous. He will work through you as you yield to Him, allowing Him to fill you and control your life. If you want to be an effective Christian, begin where the Bible says to begin: be continually filled with the Spirit. The power is already in you; it just needs to be turned on by yielding to it. Then you'll see God work through your life in a way that prepares others to receive God. Without that preparation by the Spirit—without the evidence of God in your life—you won't earn from others the right to speak about Him. If Peter had spoken without the miracles that preceded his sermon, he would have probably been stoned on the spot. Let the Spirit control your life so that you live in a way that makes others willing to hear you.

Focusing on the Facts

1. Explain what it means to be filled with the Spirit. To what is being filled with the Spirit analogous (see pp. 74-75)?
2. What does the Greek word translated "tongues" in Acts 2:4 mean (see p. 75)?
3. Using Ephesians 5:19–6:9, what is one way we can know that speaking in tongues accompanied the filling of the Spirit only at the birth of the church (see p. 76)?
4. Why did God wait until Peter and John arrived in Samaria before He baptized the Samaritans with the Holy Spirit (see p. 77)?
5. How did some Pharisees respond when Peter told them Gentiles were being baptized with the Spirit (Acts 15)? What was Peter's defense (Acts 15:7-9; see p. 78)?
6. What was the purpose of tongues-speaking recorded in Acts 8, 10, and 19 (see pp. 79-80)?
7. When the men mentioned in Acts 2:4 spoke in tongues, what were they declaring? Why (see p. 81)?
8. What was the purpose of miraculous gifts according to Hebrews 2:3-4 (see p. 81)?
9. What specifically confounded the foreign Jews (Acts 2:6-8)? For what two reasons were they surprised about the speakers being Galileans (see p. 83)?
10. Why did the Holy Spirit have the people speaking in different languages praise God? How did that help Peter's sermon, which came soon after (see p. 84)?
11. How did the crowd respond to the miraculous events recorded in Acts 2:1-11 (see pp. 85-86)?

12. Using verses from the book of Acts, tell how the callous Jews slowly worsened in their attitude toward the apostles and their followers (see p. 86)?

13. Let the Spirit _____ your life so that you live in a way that makes others willing to _____ you (see p. 87).

Pondering the Principles

1. To be filled with the Spirit is the same as letting the Word of Christ dwell in you richly (Col. 3:16). Some of the different ways you can do that are by going to a church that teaches the Bible, attending a Bible study, reading God's Word daily, meditating on what you learn from the Bible, memorizing verses, and reading good Christian books that explain how to apply Scripture to your life. Which of those things are you already doing? Are there any you're not doing that you should be? Write down the names of some Christians you know who are letting God's Word saturate their lives. How are they accomplishing that? Get together with them, and see if you can share with one another good ways to let God's Word have more influence on your lives.

2. Using your answers from the third and sixth "Focusing on the Facts" questions, how would you answer someone who says that the filling with the Spirit is always accompanied by speaking in tongues?

Scripture Index

Topical Index

filling of, 18, 67-70, 74-75, 80, 87
Old Testament ministry of, 16
permanent indwelling of, 16, 52, 57
possession of as mark of Christian, 57, 67
promise of, 15-17, 44

Inspiration, definition of divine, 46
Ishtar, 43
Isis, 43

Jesus Christ
ascension of, 29-31
earthly family of, 41-42
finished work of, 9
postresurrection appearances of, 13-14, 22
second coming of. *See* Second coming
spiritual vs. physical presence of, 14
unfinished work of, 9-10, 13
Josephus, 76
Judas
apostasy of, 36, 47, 51
early church's hatred for, 49
greed of, 47
replacement of, 37-38, 46, 49-50
suicide of, 48-49
ultimate fate of, 51-52
Judgment seat of Christ. *See* Rewards

Kingdom of God
mediatorial
church, 25
conscience, 23
government, 23-24
judges, prophets, and kings, 25

patriarchs, 24-25
millennial, 25-26
universal, 22

Lent. *See* Catholicism
Lots, 52
Luke, 8

Mary. *See* Catholicism and Jesus Christ, earthly family of
Matthias, 36-38, 49-52
McCheyne, Robert Murray, 11
Ministry
accusations against ministers, 51-52
behind-the-scene, 50-51
preparation for, 10-11
Miracles, purpose of, 81, 87
Missions. *See* Evangelism and discipleship

Nimrod, 42-43

Osiris, 43

Pentecost. *See* Church, birth of; Feasts; and Holy Spirit, baptism of
Prayer, new age of, 44-45
Prophecy
typical, 59-62
verbal, 59

Rewards, believers', 30-31

Sabbath day's journey, 39-40
Scofield, C. I., 39
Second coming
indifference toward, 26-27
preoccupation with, 27
rewards given to believers. *See* Rewards

Moody Press, a ministry of the Moody Bible Institute, is designed for education, evangelization, and edification. If we may assist you in knowing more about Christ and the Christian life, please write us without obligation: Moody Press, c/o MLM, Chicago, Illinois 60610.